Vada Pav in Mumbai

Anita Beri

authorHOUSE®

AuthorHouse™
1663 Liberty Drive
Bloomington, IN 47403
www.authorhouse.com
Phone: 1-800-839-8640

First published by AuthorHouse   02/25/2012

ISBN: 978-1-4678-7816-6 (sc)
ISBN: 978-1-4678-7817-3 (ebk)

Printed in the United States of America

A Writer's Dilemma

A writer's dilemma. I do not know about other writers, however, I am sure about one thing. People write because most of us wants to get it our of our heart and then, once its out from our heart, it almost becomes a journey and a discovery. Its almost like starting to trek the world's flora and fauna, initially it may be just for the safety to go and hide somewhere and then, its almost like once into this natures flora an fauna, one is on the most lovely journey.

Personally for me, writing is a process of cleansing my self, my thoughts, a feeling of let go and releasing and then, feeling light and exhilarated and evolving as a person, as a soul, becoming the person, God created me to be.

And I will touch upon a dilemma that I think most of the writers go thru, because I am sure, in our hearts we feel the same. The writing part is very evolving and developing and a lovely journey, its almost a drive to the inner world of ourselves and knowing and understanding more and more of ourselves, its almost like a treasure that one creates and cherishes and keeps forever, those moments and times and experiences.

Its only when someone decides to make it public to the world does a little dilemma starts and especially if the writer's work is about himself or herself. It opens her private world to the world. She may be a little vulnerable during that time and may be most of the time. At the time, the feeling of getting the work published, this feeling could be very strong within her. She may have to battle this however.

Cos she has this urge to turn to the world thru her book, leaving a message for those who seek, allowing herself to be opened up to the world, to let them know, that its okay to be yourself and just be yourself and that's the best way to live life. She may have this urge that may be some soul may be going thru the same what she went thru and hence in someway be a holding hand for that person, a holding hand that says, hey, its okay to go thru all what we go thru, and the best journey is to realize and come out of our lives which looked messy and that journey is worthwhile taking, it's the most amazing journey to take to get back to life, to get back to ones self esteem, to get back to loving oneself and respecting oneself and believing that one is worth more than what one sees at present.

The writer may have this feeling to reach out to masses and reaching out thru a book or reading may be the best way to reach out, to the unknown faces, no matter where they are, it does not matter, what skin they wear, it does not matter, what language they speak, it does not matter, what background they come from, it does not matter what culture they belong to, it does not matter where they come from, cos the language of human soul is one and the experiences that a human soul goes through does not see the color of human races or the geographies of the human voices, its one but the same. So while the writer may have this dilemma of publishing the book, yet, it's this overwhelming feeling which overtakes and then, nothing matters.

And then, that's another journey that the writer who takes, when the writer decides to publish the book itself, the writings itself.

Anita Beri, is keeping it simple, this is sure not an auto-biography but these are some experiences from her own personal life and some from her own imagination world, of her imaginative and creative life she dreams and has dreamt of.

Born in a small town of Nainital of Uttranchal state of north India, Anita grew up at different cities and then went out for her graduation and then worked in capital city and then again studies in her post graduation.

It was during her graduation second year, that she came for the very first time to Mumbai and almost instantly fell in love with the city, with the spirit of city of Mumbai, with the waves near the sea, she saw the sea for the first time at Marine Drive and almost shouted in excitement, with the streets of Mumbai, with the Locals in Mumbai with the Rains of Mumbai and during these two months of summer training for her project work, she survived on Vadapav (Indian Burger) in Mumbai, a five rupee Vadapav almost like a doughnut, a poor man's meal in US, she immediately took a liking to Vadapav and its spicy taste, relished the fresh pav (bun) with green deep fried long chilies and the cutting (half cup of tea) of Mumbai that she fell in love, to come back to work in the city and now lives in this city on the 7th floor, owns her own flat and has been working in Mumbai for seven years now.

She says living in Mumbai gave her a path to become the person, God created her to be and she is very much on that path, welcoming every experience living in this city, that's how the journey of this city, the city for her, the journey started from her twinkle in her every time you mention vadapav to her, to her it was her connect to the city, the city she connected deeply, to the spirit of this city and she salutes this city for everything the city gave her.

Anita, basically a mountain girl, this is the story of her spirit how it goes high and low with her experiences in her lifetime, how she evolves during the years ever since she was a 5 year old, she recollects her childhood, and some other parallels she draws from her life, with her philosophical journey in between her living, she says, she is through with one lifetime and that ends with this book and that she is now ready to live again and live another life, a second life-time.

It's true
When I write, may be I am explaining my self
Why my life, the way it is
Sometime my writings are an excuse to myself
Sometimes it's a revelation
Sometimes it's an accord of where my life is going, just to make me feel good
Sometimes it's a runaway from my daily deliberate task
Sometimes it's supporting me to carry me forward in life
Sometimes it helps me to clear my thoughts
Sometimes its pouring of exactly I feel
Sometimes it is, as it is
Sometimes holds me back in life
Sometimes it just clears my head
Sometimes it contains me
But, sure writing down is a struggle for me
Cos I do not know that I write to explain me whets going in life
Or I write as rescue
Or I write to simply write
Or I write to be my own religion, law and way of life
The fact that I write itself
Becomes a mountain for me, sometimes
Becomes a tunnel sometime
Becomes a ground sometimes
Becomes a ocean sometimes
Becomes a desert of sand sometimes
But I think sure it takes me through
Becoming an experience in it self

My decision to Publish

And I am writing this down, here as I am going through an internal war within myself, about coming out in public about my book, personally, I have loved Each and every experiences of writing up, of how I felt and what I felt and what I think of and how I feel about people, places, things in life.

This is something which is very personal and I started writing only from an idea of keeping it personal, something only for my eyes, someplace, where I could be so much myself, and trust me, this is my temple, or this quite place of mine has been a real solace and a savior for me.

It is this place, my window on my laptop, which has given life back to me, my belief back to me, my love back to me for myself, my respect back to me, it has given me myself back, I have not only evolved through these pages of mine, but I have also developed a life long relation with myself, and its been a wonderful journey so far. It has brought me closer to the dreams, that I have, to the my relationship with God, to the relationship of the two most wonderful human being in my life, who are my parents, to my sister and my brother, to it has also helped me to be grateful to all the human souls who have come into my life, its only when I wrote about my experience and my time that they were with me, on my journey of life, did I realize, that each and every person, experience, and moment I spend, was actually a blessing for me, for it was all cos of what was, did I become the person that I am today.

And it is during this time, for a couple of days, I have been having a silent conversation with myself, if I must or must not come out open with my small experiences in life, about my attempt to thread my life, while in this city of vadapav of Mumbai, I have been having this silent conversation, as there are some parts of my life, that my closed ones have never known, my parents have never known, how would they respond to me, would they call me again and become sad, or would they respect me for living my life all through and really know me as the person that I am, that I have become, despite all, would they respect me, for the journey I took, an internal journey, for most of us, in India, our parents do not know, what we live our lives like, here still we have tradition and we keep things to ourselves, coming from a very traditional family myself, I wonder, if my parents may come around and bless my life, cos after all little challenges, I am today a person, who feels proud of myself, cos of the relationship I have with my Allah, my God, who is so very grateful to God for choosing me to be child of my parents, will my parents feel strong for me, cos today, I feel that finally I am taking my journey, and I am on my purpose of life, still long way to go, however I can see the light in the end of this tunnel of my life, I almost feel like Alice in wonderland.

For I am writing this and publishing this book as it is, with no name change, with no alias, my story as it is . . . for tomorrow, I may be gone, my face will change, and someone else may live exactly the same life as mine, or may be today someone is living exactly the same life as I am living, my heart reaches out to all, wide and far, saying that its okay to Be, its okay to feel, what we feel, as long we love and respect and come around ourselves, the journey is worth taking and its very cleansing, like my friend always says—dude, we know what we have to fight against, it's the cleansing inside that we have to go through, cleansing of our souls, for our souls, for our body will turn to earth but our souls will live forever, our eternal energy of our souls will always be there and we have this lifetime opportunity, our present to make our soul free, our soul pure, and it only starts by allowing ourselves to go through life.

Keeping this in mind, I am publishing the "Vadapav in Mumbai" , my ode to this city of Mumbai, the city where meals can be bought for priceless five rupee of hot vadapav and cutting (half cup of tea—a slang of Mumbai), where the railway network runs like the veins in the body, where you can find traffic jams in the middle of night at andheri (a suburb in Mumbai), where you can stay alone and yet not be lonely, where the rains comes down heavily and still people are most humans, where an auto wala will still give back your last one paisa, and not act smart, where still most traditional Marathi culture prevails, where men do not look at women as objects, where festivals are celebrated with most discipline, where buses are efficient, where you can ask for directions from anyone, and people actually help you out if you are new to city, where opportunities are umpteen and where you can still have the spicy vadapav sitting in your BMWs and Pajeros, is the city of Mumbai, if Mumbai was a human being, I would have thanked for this wonderful human being for her patience and blissfulness, to have taken me under this wonderful Mumbai's Love and Care !

Mama, Papa, I love you & certainly I need your blessings and Love to go on with my life, my purpose and fulfillment for myself. Forgive me if anytime and anywhere I have made you sad anywhere, in the end this book is also for you, to tell you that daughter can not let you down, I have only got my spirit from you papa and mama and I am so blessed with that spirit.

I love you Rinki, I am blessed to have you in life and it's beyond words to express my gratitude to you.

To my brother, Bobby, I have developed respect and love for you as I grew up, you have been the rock of my life, thanks for being there for me.

And last and not the least to person who I will get married to, this is for you, my would-be life partner, as I had always thought of getting married to the person who knows me inside out, who respects me for who I am and with whom I become the best in myself and I become closer to my God, my Allah, I do not who you are, but, wherever you are, you are the one, I shall look forward to in my life, I look forward to you for being in my life so that we can bring out the best in each other and realize our purpose on this earth, to become closer to our souls. This book is also dedicated to you and to my twins, my girls, who is not on this earth now, but will come and are on their way after my marriage, my girls, this is a would-be mom, who is writing to you all. I await your presence in my life, to fill me up!

With love, to papa and mama and my grandparents, who are no more, still their soul is closer to me than ever before.

Dedicated to Papa, Mama, I thank you for giving birth to me and allowing me to Be, for my sister, my strength, My biggest Blessing of my Life, for My brother, The rock of my Life, I am so blessed to have you in my Life.

I thank Apeksha, for happening in my life, my friend, who helps Me to Be Me and my all other friends who keep me alive. Thanks for being in my Life, I love you. I thank all, who came in my life, and because of whom I am today, what I am, if it was not for you, I would not have been here typing this. Thank you all, each and every person, for coming into my life, the fact you happened in my life is what helped me TO BE. Whether you were for few days or weeks, months or few years, Thank you Once again!

I also thank my kesar and vajramma, who kept my home with good heart and love and made food for me, while I was away during most of times from my home in Mumbai and who gave me strength when expected the least and I thank my home, which is not just walls to me, it talks to me, it has been with me, day in and day out and my window from my home sweet home on seventh floor. I thank, the one who invented writing, it's such a powerful tool, it's almost a religion and even stronger than that. I thank who invented laptop, as it was my companion and it helped to bring out the best in me, and came around, when needed the most, it was this time, I evolved.

And last but not the least, my grandfather and grandmother, whose soul is so close to me than ever before and gives me strength in more ways than one can think of.

My Attempt to thread my life together

I. Rainfall

It all started with the rain coming down heavily. I had no clue of what was going to take place next. Although there was some feeling in the air. A feeling of warmth and hot tea on a rainy afternoon and watching the rain come down from the window of my boss's cabin. We picked up the tea and went inside and pulled down the curtains and opened the windows a little and stood there in silence, sipping tea and taking deep breathe breathing the nature into our bodies. There was some certain urge of getting closer to each other, I kept standing there looking at the rains outside and so did he, a little at the back to me as if he was embracing me with his arms and standing there near the window and yet not touching a bit.

Little did I know that from now on, from this moment on, I was entering into the a infinite space within me, an unknown and yet known, something that I have known inside for all these years, something only that stirred my soul holding it closer to me, the soul that was lost and was wandering for all these years. When I look back now, I became closer without ever touching was warmth, was peaceful, was of love, of love my soul was looking since zillion of years to contain my soul, his soul. Was that the moment.

I open the chapter of my life, my birth from this day when I saw him and when I realized this soul next to me. a soul so pure that snow could not touch it, a soul so unnerving that nature could not dither it, a soul so complete that I was completely taken by it.

II. And perhaps there are no coincidences in life

And perhaps there are no coincidences in life, even the book that you read and the people that you come across and even the hair style that you wear. I am so happy and glad to have come across all the books that I have read so far, today I sit near my window, with the most amazing sunshine and the most beautiful greenery I saw in so many years, bathing in sun and glowing in its full glory, the ground is ready to be walked on with warmth on its ground, the birds flying in a sort of ballet together, worth playing a music in the background to give that effect, the breeze blowing in and touching my window and dropping inside to touch my face and skin, brings in a little cold with it and embraces the warmth on my skin, leaving me completely refreshed.

I read the book and life of Lance Armstrong who bounced me back in my life, sitting here in my window and in past read Abraham Linchon, who taught me simplicity and the works of Paulo Coelho, who gave me dreams and importance of instincts and Pt. Nehru, who stole my heart and mind and Dr. Brain Weiss who gave me believe and love for my own life and my loved ones and so many more in the between . . . and here I sit and reflect whatever we do in our lives is purely out of the choices that we make and how we want things to shape up in our lives.

There is nothing called chance or rut-of-life or landing-in-a-situation, or even to say getting stuck in life. In the long run, we are where we are cos we decided to be in that position, consciously or sub-consciously. It is always a choice to be happy or not. It's always a choice to love oneself or abuse.

One more thing, three days back I came from Delhi from Auto Expo Show and was parked there for 7 days . . . when I landed back in Mumbai, I was not too good, I was feeling mixed. It was that moment I decided to treat me as sweet child of mine and things changed after that. Whenever I feel low and think that things needs to be changed within me and on the outside, I look at myself as mother holding her child or teaching her to walk or even taking her to school and my whole feeling towards myself changes and is changed. I feel so loved towards myself and that I need to take care of my feelings and what I am aiming to do or even what I eat and how never ever to let my self hurt me or make me down in life. I have to come around and take care of me and accept the way I am and think ahead of life what it could be.

Sometimes it intrigues me to think why have a goal or for that case what is the purpose of our lives when once we take birth. I could sit on my window the whole day and look at ground and trees and pigeon flying by, or climb up the mountain or walk in the jungle, watch the sea waves against the sands and sun glittering over it, or even just caress the horses and elephants and talk to them and I could go on and on talking about it my whole life, may be I am exaggerating, or may be I could do this forever, going from the alps to the Niagara fall to the desert to the mountain streak to the valley of flowers and yet in the end I will have so many more places and seasons and grass to touch and feel and write and talk about and picture them.

For what nature can bring in to my life and teaches me and marvels me and exalts me and leaves for more hunger in me, is unparallel. The education that I received in school or engineering or business management is so very minuscule before what nature teaches me, perhaps that's why in old civilization, people were more wise and lovable, cos they learned from nature and seasons and trusted their senses and could even read the coming of life.

I have these thoughts running in my mind, as I gather all the material I need to file a petition for divorce coming week, a day after the 26th Jan the republic day, I wonder if the falling of the date has some meaning.

I look at my wedding picture and I look at myself, I have forgotten the day and celebration, but just one feeling, I knew that I was looking the most stunning that I have ever looked in my whole life and I felt good about myself, may be I married just for the feeling, just for that moment, cos, moments are what I cherish in my life and moments are what I live for, for they form a beads in my life and I pick up the best moments of my life to thread them together and wear around my neck, touching my heart and making me feel beautiful about myself . . . that Red color wedding dress and that make up I was given, made my marriage complete, and I had got married for that feeling, time when I was over with that and I knew deep down in my heart that this marriage is not for lasting, I decided to call it off, cos for me my life and my experience and who I share it with was the most important and somehow I was sure right from the beginning that this is not for lasting.

Infact, I had fallen in love and had a life inside me too, it's a different thing I could not keep that life in me, may be I was studying that time and didn't have the job, or may be it was the weird societal reason, I decided to separate my conceived life from me even before my own life could breathe in my womb and come out as a labor of my love. I was married already, it's a different thing, this was a marriage of two minds and souls and bodies, and so here I was, trying to get married and have a surrogate for my partner, my love . . . which was so strange on the outside and inside too that I finally decided to call it off, for I couldn't be living with such a split in my mind.

I had wanted to be good to my marriage and wanted to give it the best, as an Indian bahu, however it was not for lasting. I have no regrets for the marriage and for coming out of it, I am rather happy, cos it gave me a chance to dress up in the most beautiful way that a woman could be, and I am glad that this marriage happened, cos it only re-enforced my belief in what I had sub-consciously believed in. I always saw visually as a single staying up in my home driving a Pajero to buy vegetables, looking outside my window to the green ground and somewhere this picture sees me with a child, the most beautiful child of the God within myself, cos I am nature and mother earth and I will have my progeny after me.

For me it never occurred what institutions of marriage is, why stay in the way you are expected to stay in or even work in a way you are expected to work in. Although sometimes there is a dichotomy in myself for being so ideal in a work, or relationship or anything that I do, that it kills me and suffocates me, as my space and freedom, my expression is much more dear to me than anything else. Also, I live my minute and instinct and how I feel about anything, if its gives me happiness I am there and if does not make me happy I am out of that place or moment.

It's same with people, if I love talking or being around with anyone, I will go all my way and stay up there and if it does not, I switch off. I do not mind rubbing my legs in my formal pants against the person I like and admire, it makes me happy and I receive reciprocation. This may not be forever, but until I am happy, I pursue this. I love sitting around the sea face until it fills up my mind, body and soul. I love to adventure until it scares me off, but I will go a little farther to see how far it can get.

I love talking and having a little crush over men I like, who somehow happen to be genuine kinds or successful kinds, sort of having a gall in them to do what it takes to, and I do not mind making it known to them, that I like them and have a fantasy over them. Its a different thing I may not go that far with them to caress a little more intimately with them, cos that switches me off. Lately it does. Unlike my other days when I was in school or college or even first few years of my working. I would fall in so called love with men of all ages, my ages or even younger to me and go all out to be a perfect lover and friend and finally end up in bed and that was the end of it. When in bed, I got to know them better, it's strange only when you get physical with men, you know where they are coming from, who they are and sure you know who you are looking for and for me it was always not the person, I was, so-called falling in love, with.

But sure, I enjoyed having to make love in the most wild manner, in the most exotic place I could think of and in the most weird way, like stealing away from my home at 2 in the night and climbing a wall to first floor and make love in the moon light and lie down in peace and come back to my home, by hanging myself in a sheet tugged into a rope like and climbing down like sheet of rope, it, I believe gave me a kick, as I would feel like out from a comic of phantom, I fancied over and I think it had a deep wild impact on me a child, as I loved the stores of phantom and possibility even fancied him for my love.

I used to get caught over my teenage mischief and also used to get beating for same. It so happened once that I told my mother at age of 17 that I think I am pregnant and my periods are not coming. That was the first time; my mother clinically told me how does one get pregnant. Still for the fear of getting it over with, we went for a test and I was clean chit, for I could not have got conceived, when the person held me on the outside and touched my uppers tenderly. But I did not know, I thought just sleeping with an opposite make one have a child.

Looking back I had quite a lot of fun I believe. However I was now so used to the idea of getting caught over anything, that I started liking that feeling and sooner or later I would sub consciously do things and go over this feeling again and again just to have that feeling again and again Now when I look back at life so far, I see that I was playing this game again and again with myself and I enjoyed it, deep down, however hard I may cry on the outside.

Sometimes my logic defies my education and my belief in principal of cause and effect. when I look back to my life, I believe I did everything, whether it was studies and getting good grades or winning a sprint or growing flowers in my garden or having a silent deep long crush with brushes of getting physical with him by sitting closer to him, my uncle who was 10 years older to me, or even running away to my boy friends to the terrace and trying the first kiss or get closer, or burning mid night oil to pass engineering exam in the hot summer night when all were asleep or wearing a lovely revealing skirt or frock that my mom would stitch for me, I loved doing all this, cos I just loved doing it and that's it. There is no other explanation to it. This is how I see it as today. However few years back, I saw myself a perfect case for the psychotherapy and someone who was emotionally drained or someone, who missed out on love in life. I even went to meet a person who deals with all this and after having spend time with her for an hour; I decided never ever to consult any other human being for my well being.

I am my own master and I decide what I want I want in life. Its me who decides whether I want to be happy or not. It's always a choice of an individual and there is always a way out. It also has something to do with accepting oneself as one is. Allowing one to be what one is, without attaching any pre cursors or any qualifications. To be comfortable with what one is deep down inside. And may be that's why the banner of my hand phone say "Be Yourself"

Cos no matter what age we are I think, it not correct to say, that one is young or old, or one is small or has grown up. I personally think that we are all in our full potential and full capacity whether we are a child of 6 months or 1 yr or 8 years, or 17 years or 30 years. Our senses are as alive as any seasons or the sun shining and we know deep down what is what. Most importantly we do things that give us happiness and take away any pain from us or protects, for this is an animal instinct, which Homo sapiens have and cannot be denied. Its black or white when it comes to being happy. It's a different thing some of our fellow beings inflict pain upon themselves to get going, but again, it's a decision that one takes consciously.

And in this course of life, I also learned that self pity is not going to take one any where, but only worsens life that could be, and that every experience of my life, when I look back and look forward to only makes me feel good that it happened, cos it made me the person that I am today and I could not have had such a beautiful mind if it was not for the experiences of life that it gave me. Yes, may be I sound very narcissist when I say that I have a beautiful mind, it is because I believe, I have and who knows better than myself. Its an extension of saying that I am my own beautiful child.

And when ones gets to accept that there was no rights and wrongs in life, life becomes much more simpler and one has to less thinking about anything, for thinking sometimes could paralyze ones brain and thinking leads to opiniating anything or judging anything.

Its not simple to get to the level of accepting the way things are or the way one is, it takes work and deliberate effort to do this, not just for oneself, however for fellow beings too or for anything, cos human mind tends to be more benevolent to self than to any one else.

Somehow I believe that thinking is a powerful tool when it is used as reflecting on something, cos it brings us revelations rather then opinion or judgment. Some English words must be disappeared from the dictionary like—judging or opinion, as they create value based ideas and the word "Value "is such a misnomer today. In our values there is nothing right or wrong, it is what we value and is close to our heart and would vary from one human being to another, so where does the question of value based idea or even judgment come. It is very subjective.

For me my marriage was for that moment and it was over before it began. For someone else marriage is a life and life long association, for another it is winding of a relationship from a previous birth. I do not know, however, all is okay and I say it as I have learnt to accept it the way it is from the inside and not from the outside.

And it darns me to have my own child and care for. I may not need to get married or even have a physical intimacy with a man, as today I can have my child without having to do anything, but just conceiving clinically. It may sound too straight and clinical, but I am excited to hear the good news that now I can have my own child without having to go through something or any attachments I do not want in my life. For me having my child is the prime important, the institutions come later, cos I know that love survives everything and I know having to raise your own self in another form cannot be that bad.

I do not know how important it is have a father to the child, but I believe that love is more important and the child needs that more than anything else.

The sociological aspect is something what human being created for a better securer environment and a better care, however when this factor is itself in question or has outgrown, I do not see the need of conformity for the same.

I know one thing and have learned it too, if you stay long enough you will swim through and only if you stick out your head out of anything, you will finally be able to stand on your own, no matter what. Just keep your head up, held high and your heart with you.

III. If you even have the thought in your mind

If you even have the thought in your mind, then somewhere you are prepared for it, cos no thought ever comes to mind, if your heart and soul are not ready for the same.

How many times in my own life have I wondered and pondered upon anything that would happen only to me and take away my happiness and would happen again and again, it was only when I realized that I was sub consciously making things happen in my life the way I wanted my life to go. And once I knew this, it took two things to take this forward, one is to accept my life the way it went, cos going back was not possible, but rather to accept that I wanted the way things are deep down inside me and second was now to chart the life that I fancied and dreamed of. And once I took this, I am like a person in a boat rowing my own boat and I knew which direction I had to oar my boat, times when I could not, I would just flow along the current, however, mostly I would decide which direction to take next, however horrifying it could be for the next person or any other boat passing by.

Sometimes I am very varying to tell others what I dream of, they are very dear to me and when I share my dreams with other people, they see it from their light. I dream of grape Farms, with horses and a school for riding, with my chopper, if I need to go somewhere and my baby with me. I have a friend of mine who visits us regularly and I have a home facing the sea. My paintings are up on the exhibition and my book is already published along with the pictures I click. Whenever

I have shared this with more than my friends who I love and other way round, other has always given what they think of whole thing. This might truly dampen ones spirit.

I had always dreamt myself sitting with a laptop in a coffee bar and typing away to glory. I was at that time not very sure why I wanted one; however I visualized myself with it. A very close friend of mine actually mocked the whole idea and told me to have purpose focus in my life. What good is it to have the laptop and do what with it . . . years later I bought one and today my laptop is a way out, is my freedom, my sheet of expression for myself and is my partner in all the times. It's an asset for me and my life, when one is around, my laptop comes around and I type furiously, to feel better, to feel lighter, and to feel loved, and to feel expressed.

I have learnt that writing or any form of expression is the first step to acknowledge one's existence and one's being. may be that why in the ancient times, we see so many caves and walls and structure with paintings and some writings on them, that was their way of expression of how they felt and how life was then . . . my laptop is my wall of the my cave and I paint on it and write on the same. When sometimes I am doing that and is either happy and not so happy, I lie down looking at the walls of my cave and absorb the paintings and feel good about myself. Whatever I visualize I never undermine that, cos I know now that there is a purpose being it, it may not be so clear in the beginning however, when one stays around ones dreams and move towards the same, the goal or purpose starts to get clearer. Its like some moving force or hand moving you closer to the purpose for what you are born, and the force behind it is love.

Love is a such a strong emotion, the love of anything,. of writing, of painting, of nature, of children, loving itself and I keep this love intact in my heart to keep me loved all the time and guard against any force other than love, around me and that makes all the difference.

I do not know much about spirituality and God, but it intrigues me know more and more about the finer human beings who existed at one point of time. I cannot go back to the times when Prophet Mohammad (SAW) was born or Christ existed but sure I can know about their lives and the purpose they had.

The more I read about Allah, Islam, Bhagwat Gita and my faint reading on other religion, I feel something powerful and serene that lifts my belief and sometimes makes me feel so normal, cos I find that they were very normal human being but for one thing, I see that they had integrity and that was the biggest asset and that is what created religion. The uncorrupted and pure mind, the minds which did no harm to anyone is what distinguished them all the time.

The biggest asset that all had in common was the consistency and all this lead to a straight line always with no wavering and people needed straight lines in their lives to keep going. Like when I waver I return to my readings, my Islam, My Gita, My Allah and anything so pure, so untouched and so straight is what is religion for me. If it is dirty, I need to clean it. If it is wavers, I need to follow my straight line to keep it simple and that's my religion.

May be religion is geometry. The straight line between any two points. the line is consistent and clear, no broken lines, no curves and the line consists of many points and when joins each points a line is created, a message that all are equal and all deserve same treatment when one lives ones life and all have equal opportunities. The discipline of straight line. Geometry is scientific and that's why the relation of science and religion. In ancient times, when pyramids evolved and sun dial was created, the concept of time came and works of physics evolved, no wonder had a deep sense of something more powerful, which human being named as God, Allah, Messiah and their works progressed so intensely in the discovery of forces of Nature and existence.

IV. Mutual Divorce

Sometimes It intrigues me that there is nothing called a mutual anything . . . mutual agreement or mutual understanding or anything for that case. I feel that this term is somewhere a disconnect, as there has to be a difference of opinion and difference when any two entities are concerned without which any existence is possible. It is only out this that any balance is achieved too.

Science talks about the gravitational pull and it is that there are weak forces and there are strong forces and hence somewhere due to pull and push of forces there is a balance maintained. It is so with any entity or living being. Sometimes I think that everything is a living being as everything has an effect on nature and Nature is the mother of all Living, the Melting Pot, where everything came out from and where everything goes into. A plastic bag has a humongous affect on nature and so does the molecule with a nucleus in it.

While filing for my divorce, which we call mutual, I think is called mutual, because both parties are at the least talk to each other and try and come to a common point, however to think that mutually agreed divorce is possible is only a fools paradise. It defies the logic that if there were no difference why at all one would have decided to separate, I wonder how can it be called a mutual divorce. I totally disagree to this and the demon is to play under or work under the pretext that divorce is mutual because it sends wrong connotations and wrong perception, wrong expectation. It is only when I am going through what in the law is termed a mutual divorce is when I am realizing how misleading this term "mutual" is in general and more in so specifically.

There would be a difference of opinion and there has to be, cos if difference do not occur, existence is not possible. Then it would be a dead walk and dead existence all over. This is nature and to have difference is natural and I believe is the reason for survival and existence.

The differences is essential to have civilizations, and changes in progress of the era, differences is essential to thrive economy and difference is essential to have standing of the nations and oceans and sea and mountains and desert and green lands and forests.

Difference is the essence of nature and yet seamlessly unites the nature and holds it together. Cooperation exits only when there is a difference in the first place. It could be difference of opinions or economy, the abundance or shortage of something, difference at any level and therefore cooperation. May be in dictionary the meaning of mutual should be cooperative difference which sends right signal to mind and prepares one accordingly. For me, in my divorce it sends signal that we have and had differences and now we are cooperating to come to an agreement. Whether agreement leads to what results is a different subject altogether.

V. Succumb to your weakness and it will go

I had one thought troubling me and deciding my choices and reactions since I was a little child. I liked this uncle of mine a lot and I remembered him hugging me when I was a child, a girl of 5 year old and throwing all tantrums to go to school. This uncle of mine used to visit us, he used to skate and I was totally enthralled by the fact and seeing those wheels in the shoes.

I was very excited at the fact and very impressed with this uncle of mine. And who says that kids are small and do not understand any thing. I really liked this uncle of mine and I knew I was his favorite kid, until he saw me growing as a teenager in my full bloom. And I knew that he did notice me growing up to be a wild teenager. We have a difference of ten years almost and somehow when you grow up the age difference emotionally vanishes.

Physically too, once, you have monthly natural cycle coming, a girl ceases to be a girl anymore and becomes a woman, young lady inside and is ready for anything in life. The maturity starts setting in. The hugging in of that uncle of mine had made such a long lasting impression on me that somewhere I used to sub consciously look for that feeling, very warm and someone older holding you like a baby that I was at that time. This feeling just grew deeper in me as I grew up. I have no idea if he felt the same, or he held me like a kid when I was so very small, may be he just loved me as a kid and played with me like a child. However, we both noticed the feeling when we both grew up.

He went through rough in life, he did not receive so much love and respect and hope from his parents which he did from my father, and that's why he liked coming to our place and I always understood that. Being small, I liked him as a person and believed that he is made to be his best in life and hoped that he did his best in life and not get depressed by what others think. Cos I remembered that feeling when he used to hug me close tight, he made me feel good and loved by someone who is older and it was pure love and I thought someone who could be good at heart, can't be so bad in life.

However as I grew up in midst of my school and studies and family, life went on like a cruise, with so many things happening, crushes for boys, I hid all that and made up for all that by good in studies, it was a pure barter system, I knew I could only hide my feelings and my mischief and would be forgiven a little only if I am doing good at studies and in school and I also quite likes the praises and honors at school and I enjoyed the likeness of everyone towards me at home, family, grandparents and at school and then, it grew on me. I used to be on extremes, either I would only study like hell or just go out and have fun and play and cycle or flirt with boys.

One thing I knew deep down in my heart, I was always fighting against myself to be a better person and always taking risks and out of curiosity to know what it felt like being held by a boy of my age and what was is it likes to have been kissed for the first time. It excited me a lot. My first crush was when I was a six year old. I still remember, my brother's friend, he used to come to our place to play, typical boys play. He used to wear a dark red blazer at that age a year older to me and used to wear black shoes and used to look so good. If I was 19 and he was 20, I am sure we would have been dating.

And so life went on. My escapades with curiosity as a growing teenager and my extreme about studies lead me to engineering college. The thing that drove me to engineering college was I wanted badly to get out of home. I guess with all other factors at home, it basically came from a feeling of attaining my freedom and free space. The idea of hostel excited me more than becoming an engineer. Of course, if I wanted my freedom, I had to work and to pay for it, incidentally made me work very hard, it was not studies, it was the idea of freedom and being on my own, which made me study in hot summer late night, solving math problems keeping my towel on notebook, so that the sweat does not make my notebook wet, I slogged like a donkey and I was there two months later celebrating my freedom, in the hostel of my engineering college and wood and river that engulfed my college. I was happy in life and in my own space.

And somehow, I love going through an emotional upheaval and even if it is some silly girl stuff. It made me feel important in life; cos now I had other things to worry other than studies to keep my mind occupied most of the time. Sometimes I was as free a bird, cos my college was in middle of woods and rivers and large farms and tribal and I felt that I so much belonged to this place. It would fill me up walking in those woods and sitting by that river in sunny afternoon, looking at the shimmering river waters and just lie down there or even hop across the boat and cross the river. Little did I know that coming to that place, that campus was the birthplace of the person, I was becoming to be. I loved nature and I was at the right place. Studying engineering was only incidental and then I had my best of friends.

I was like a bird who had got out cage and wanted to go all out and taste life, everything. I was in a hurry and I could have been in my dangerous sprits. I was the most adventurous 360 degrees in life and I did everything a 19 year old in any other country like US was doing.

I was suppose to be in love with a Police Officer and I was going through a very intense physical relationship with a kind of psycho from my batch, we used to travel together from place of study in that town to our respective home town. He was in deep trouble he told me and used to face hallucinations and knew what future was coming and had trouble at home and I had all the heart to be his good friend and I would go any limit to make him feel good, any limit.

My instincts same as with my uncle was working on me, little did I know. Anyway, it was all over in first semester and second semester I started fresh, leaving behind all that happened. My good friends knew about it and had kept mum about it and it became quite a joke. Something even I could laugh about however serious it may seem when I was in it. Is it not strange when we are into something, why we cannot see the bigger picture, it's like the color on canvas, a red color or then green color, but only when other sees the whole canvas, that person knows what the painting is like?

Another four years were great at college. I supposed to be fallen in love again and again and had great friends. There was time I used to be on my own, completely on my own, all alone. I had loved these times, for reasons I do not know.

Time at college ended to see me working in Delhi and it was a corrupted freedom space I knew in my heart. Another break up supposedly tore my world apart and I fell in love again and another break up again, saw me landed at home after 2 and half years of working in Delhi.

I am using the word supposedly fallen in love. I guess I never fell in love with anyone. I was only dramatizing falling in love. I was only copying what my good friends were going through, stable relationships ending up in marriage and I felt left out, and so I was supposedly falling in love, going steady and when I would discover that it was more of a reaction deep down, I would work on a break up, cos deep down in my heart, I would only expect that to happen and then the whole drama after that, I would say. But seriously enough, I was surprised that I was being very very serious when all this was going on. I was serious in playing it out and seriously believing that I was in love and I would do anything for the other person to make the relationship at its best.

Little I was forgetting that the most important person in any relationship is I and I was paying least attention to that. Some weird Indian movies made me think when you fall in love you do everything for other person, what a fart how much I wonder it must have effected other girls life too. It's called poisoning effect from songs and Indian movies.

However I would always bounce back at life, you know why cos deep down, I still had not found what I was truly looking for and therefore what I was going through did not matter. I was looking for may be a purpose in my life, I was doing anything to find that, anything . . . dangerous too. I was looking for love and I went to bed with married men. I was looking for security and I sozzeled with rum and coke with the company of the most wretched men, who you know did what after I was drunk and I quite liked it too. I enjoyed it, cos I thought that is security and belonging to someone, being someone. I lost my virginity and lost my innocence.

I went out and out with the man, I used to be in awe of and I gave furiously, to get what I was looking for. I had almost become a desperate and lost my good friends. No one wanted to quite talk to me cos they knew by my body language. However few good friends paid me visit and loved me as a person I was and helped me get out of it. I inherently knew what was good for me and what was bad and somehow I knew where to stop anything and quit it.

I was reacting; I was wild like a fire and was determine to correct my life. Yet again, I fell in love finally I thought, only to know it was not love, but a way to keep my belief that goodness prevails and that love exists. ha. I broke up and saw me at my home, leaving the city of wretched freedom and now was with my parents and brother and sister, and was at peace and was happy again.

I had grown over this period of time. I knew more, have seen more, and had gone through more than I thought I would be at age of 25. It's when I decided to do another studies to change my life and get going in life. Somehow, studies always had a cleansing effect on me and always helped to get better and calmer. I studies sociology during at stay at home and it had profound effect on me. I studies history and I liked it. Somewhere I was going through metamorphosis and I was realizing it too.

However two years of college saw me getting together with someone, who I had fantasized for long long time and I believed that it could not be a coincidence about having this person here. We got talking, we got close, very very close, we became, good friends, we liked each other and we were living together.

However I was not ready to believe from my past experience that this was my guy and we could get married. I only thought that one day he would leave too like many other.

Someone said correct, you get what you expect. I was expecting getting hurt by this person and hurting in return, I took out my all childhood and teenage and college un-satiated feelings and hurt on this one person. This was the most intense relationship I was going through with my insecurities in my peak. Would he marry me, would he not? He had a girl and was going to get married, he told me later, and this (I) was just time-pass. I was back to my insecure self and now finding potential husbands for self and would come back and tell him everything. He was a control freak and very very possessive in beginning. I would anything to find out another guy for me and thus again I was in my dual relationships trip and I would feel the most guilty. I do not know if I was sub consciously creating this. I guess you head for what you want deep down. I was too. However we both continued and spend more and more time with each other.

Physically we had nothing left to be unturned with each other One year of college and then working in Mumbai, we became a pest for each other. Could not stay without each other, but somewhere we both were not committed to each other. This person was my sound board for my entire life. His inherently inquiring nature got my whole life exposed to him from a two yr old of my age until that moment.

Until one day as I was growing to be of now urgent marriage age and had to get settled. I called him what he had to say on this, when I went to meet a guy like in a typical Indian arranged marriage. He said he had nothing to say and I could do what I wanted to. Out of reaction I said yes and got married and was determined to come out.

You know what the biggest secret of my marriage is I got married just out of my reaction and separation was inevitable. I did all that in reaction to that one phone call, to everything we had in between. And maybe I always thought that I wanted to be a divorcee and then get married again, this was my thought as I was growing up from 20 to 21 years old, when in my first job, my aim was to be a divorcee. And have some 2-3 marriages. I do not know where this idea came from, but I can sure tell, to get to where you want to be, good or bad, it's true, the power of visualization is very very true, you see you life in colors and in pictures and then, sub consciously it seeps in and comes true.

Toady, I am sitting here separated four years and paying for what I never intended to, paying for my freedom, my space. But during this course of life I learned one thing that it pays to dream and think positive and dream positive and focus on oneself and be very very selfish. I learned when you do not love yourself, you cannot love anyone else. When you cannot take care of you, you cannot take care of any one else. If you do not respect yourself, you do not respect anyone else. If you cannot forgive yourself, you cannot forgive anyone else.

If you do not decide to move over your past and leave the bagagges behind, you cannot expect other to progress, if you do not decided to be happy yourself, you cannot expect give happiness to anyone else. If you stop judging yourself, you will stop judging other too. It is all about the person and has nothing to do with outside world.

And I am glad that I reached this point today and am working on myself. I am glad that I dream for me today and live for me today. I am glad like one of my dear friend says;—you have conquered your demons and are at peace with them.

I am surprised at myself that I no longer so easy for anyone. I respect and love myself today, the way I am. I am okay with getting close to my uncle at and getting over the feeling of him holding me close. I did that, and now it does not matter. The thoughts do not matter any more and do not chase me sub consciously anymore, which had been since I was five year old. I choose to get over with it and the best way was to do what I desired to do all these years. I am glad I am through with it. Clinically and now it's over. I feel much above the ground after that and I am at peace with myself and even with him today. I can talk normal now.

Seems like I took a full circle to get close to me and now I am with myself. And when I look back, I never regret, cos I would have got where I am today, if it was not for what I went over. And it would be in correct to say, if it was good or bad what I went through, cos every experience brought its learning's and carved for what I am today.

Sometimes I wonder, what saints are like and now it does not disturb or surprises me to think, that after possibly what they went through, seeing all colors of life and tasting everything, and having done all that, why they come a full circle and then can look at life dispassionately and yet feel above everything.

It's like in nature, the heat, steam and clouds, wind, pouring down, being in sea and mud and decomposing and going over the cycle and heat and then returning to the sky, where you could look back and appreciate what you went through and not underestimate or over judge the power of complete cycle. The feeling is spiritual and I feel as if I am the chosen one by God.

VI. As I come closer to my dream

As I come closer to my dream, I become clearer. It is such a different experience to work when your dream is clear. I have been working in the corporate scene for last 7 years put together. However, when I walk into my office, my, the thoughts that run in me so very different. I know that rest of people and each, most of the soul on my working floor, would be working, getting up in the morning and coming to work day after.

May be God had a plan for each, however, it so much true how much do we listen to our heart. and one is so very true that no matter what one's dream is, a dream is a dream and when most of the people hear it, may ridicule it, and at times we get lead by such people, however always remember and I am doing a loud thinking that always keep your dream close to your heart and respect your dream, for it is only your heart truly knows what you desire and no one else has an iota of idea about what you desire in your heart, truly, deeply, madly.

You know what, work will go on, like in my international marketing, markets will keep opening and the excitement will go on, however there will be a time when one will get bored of same kind of excitement. Market will open, launches will happen and sales will pluminate and brand will get established. however what about one's own self brand, what about ones own dreams . . . I will have my own chopper one day, I will travel the whole world, I will drive a pajero, I will have my own grape farms, I will open a riding school and create an institute. What about the plan God made for you.

And you only live life once and there is no second chance, People who believe in second chance while they have the opportunity in their hands, there and then, are blinded by the noise of the world and are not able to differentiate what their heart is telling them, cos they are so louded by the conditioning they are receiving, they cannot hear what their heart desires and therefore they talk and utter same from their words.

And while I am currently going through this metamorphosis, I believe in one more thing to mention worthwhile here. Remember God has a plan for you and all one had to follow omens. I truly believe in that. It is very strange I had always visualized myself as a single, I never saw any one else in my plans, it is very strange, however it is true, how do I even tell my own mother that in my whole life, I also cannot see the other person as a spouse, but yes, I see the person, who I love and respect and who gives me freedom and who believes in my freedom and believes in my living life fully, completely, with all my heart.

Looking back into my life, I see the events following, and happening, came out of home, to college and then capital city and then to Mumbai, all this journey made the person that I am today, there was so much of cleansing that needed to happen that I had travel this distance and meet the person with whom, I could held my head with and talk shoulder to shoulder with.

Along, this journey, I tied the knot and broke out of it and then I came into family of Jim and Nancy Dornan and Staffan and Naina and Ramdas. I have learnt humongous from these human beings. Staffan, my mentor, for whom i have respect next to my grandparents and parents, came into life when I was looking out for hope and he gave me hope to live my own life and thus started my journey towards my own life.

Before this I was living for someone else and what other thought me of. It is through the training programs and tapes that I learnt not to give up on my goals and stay away from the negative.

It is during this journey that I landed into the wild animal whose spirit was as free as me and I was one with this creature. I started horse riding and in this journey I realized my dream. More than that, I realized that this will help me becoming the best of human being in me.

It will help me becoming the best God has created me to be. I also came across my guru, for whom I would actually dedicate my riding too. I own my riding it to him, it is with him that I started thinking to take riding into an institutional level in my home country. Now I am not a revolutionary, may be my thoughts are. However this is what I really believe in my heart. May be this journey has a meaning for me.

It is strange when I look back some five years, I think I was not prepared to even thinking of going out of this country. I was so very vulnerable and so very emotionally weak, that I could not have survived in the atmosphere. Now, it is these five years that have made me the person and being able to take care of myself.

Yes, it is true, nothing in life ever goes waste, you are always becoming the person you want to be, if that is so much in your sub conscious level. And also that every experience counts, because God plans everything. The challenges one has on one's way, after a period of time when we look back we thank God that Good lord something like that happened in our life and therefore today I am better equipped to handle this situation in life. So every experience counts, each and every. We cannot weigh something as more or less. For it is these small things in life that makes larger goals simpler and reachable in life.

Trust on God and oneself comes with practice and deliberation. However it is one of the simplest things. Here all one has to do is tell oneself and remind oneself of ones dream and believing in God that He has a plan and he is testing you for before he actually gives you that reward to test your worthiness. To accomplish this, one need to keep one's eyes on the goals and just go over the mundane, like to keep driving in traffic even when the traffic is bad or good, one keeps driving and keeps going, to reach home.

VII. More than what it appears to be

Something more than just wanting to do something inside me is revolting inside me. It is not about leaving the corporate world forever and it's not about having my own grape farm all this is symbolic. The corporate world is symbolic and so is my retaliation to it. And similarly the grape farm is symbolic and so is my flying towards it. However we live real lives and so we have a need to represent what we live for and what we die for. It is simple as that. We wear what we feel deep down inside and we utter how we feel about ourselves. We live our lives the way we deep down want out lives to be and we respond to others in the manner we respond to our selves and our being and existence.

My retaliation from the corporate world is wanting to leave the world where the realization is, that, this is not freedom; this is slavery in the highest form. I work for someone else and may be in the process help the other that one person's dream to come true. May be at this crossroads I cannot see that following this path may not lead me to my dreams and my time is running out. My retaliation from the corporate world is that, it is a form of exploitation, a trade for my time, for money that I receive in return. In this jungle of corporate I see some internal motives of people, some act of scene only for the heck of it; I am not able to see honesty and freedom.

I, flying away to grape farm is the symbol of something that belongs to me and me alone. It's a symbol of me getting married to nature and taking care of it with my hands. It is a symbol of me having nature as my child and nurturing it, watering it and even before all this, keeping the cot ready for my baby to come and take birth and grow and bloom in sun and rains. It is a symbol of giving my love to nature and filling my eyes with its freshness and fullness.

And maybe at this stage it has to do with my state of divorcing, when I see no reason and no logic of closing this chapter and yet I see that person is taking his sweet time and holding up, the divorce process, only for the heck of holding up, for the want of taking some sweet revenge, I fail to understand the human logical mind and his natural sense of progression. It does not really matter to me anymore, for when the person who never stayed in my life, there is no question of him going away. He was never there.

However, may be the arrangement of marriage and getting some title in society has affected me somewhere. I am amazed at the irony of how can the nuptial ties can even effect someone when one's mind body and soul are not there in the ties, still it effects and that's reality.

I sometimes wonder what I would have done if I was the at the persons place. For one thing I know that when love and belongingness and wanting to belong never existed and a urge to become someone's close never existed nor was ever emerged, how, on earth can I have the right on some ones life, I would rather let it go and free myself and other person as soon as possible, for there is so much more to life. For this may be the beginning of what I call my opening the door of my dreams.

For nothing is easy, neither remaining in a marriage where there is no love or wanting to, coming out of the very very plastic formal wedding lock, which never existed in the first place. Only if freedom was easier, lock up of free will would have never existed in the first place.

However hard life may seem and however hard and harsh people may seem to be, I think we always have a choice to absorb it or let it not effect us. Even if it does, we have a choice to distract our minds from the likes of it or to remain with it. And that in real sense is called free will, to be able to choose what resides in our mind body and soul and what not. And free will is also the acknowledgment of which side to look, we can look back or we can look forward and it is only upon an individual to be able to take that decision.

Always, for nature also knows how much hard to bite in cold, when the person has decided to enjoy the cold breeze and not feel attacked by same. For a person can always decide how to feel about anything and I think that in real sense is called free will.

Free will is not about the freedom to do what one wants to do and how one wants to do, but free will is the starting point, it is the birthplace, of, as soon as a person starts looking at choices and possibilities. Yes, free will may lead one to freedom, or it can also lead one to the other path. For one can still have a free will while remaining in an arranged wedlock, on the other hand, one may still not have a free will even after coming out of the state of wedlock.

Coming back to my response to the work that I choose and my urge to have my own grape farm is my urge for love, for loving, for caring, for recognition, for belongingness, complementing my being.

VIII. If tears flow, let them river your pillow

If tears flow, let them river your bed, in this river you will not drown, but only you will float and you will be lighter and lighter and then you can fly away. If you feel guilty a bout something, weep it and take it out of your system.

And no matter how hard I am from the outside, I know that in this marriage of mine, I have not been on the right path. I was going thru something I was not able to handle and my love was not able to handle and I screwed up my life in the process, I broke someone's faith in the process, someone's faith in marriage, someone faith in wife, ones partner in life, someone's faith in loving someone's, he loved me dearly and was happy and I in the process of my illusion of love and not being able to live with my love, I broke someone's else's love. I acted in haste and I acted in anger, I acted in impatience, I acted in disgust, I acted out of love, I acted out having lost love, I acted out of skin closes ness to someone and yet not being able to come out of it, I acted in childlike manner, I acted in not being to come to reality. I acted in my best capacity. I acted without thinking what I was doing to other person. I acted taking my anger on the other person.

It was my revolt on what we call as arranged marriage. How on earth who does not know you can love you and keeps you and get married to you. I was angry, not on person, however on the whole system of families and institute of arranged marriage.

My anger however killed someone's faith who had come from a very different background, very traditional thinking and it broke him and I knew that it broke him completely to never believe in another woman, to never trust another woman, to never look at another woman, to never think of coming close to another woman, for the man I got married to thought that wife is what love is, wife is what a friend is, wife is what a confidant is, wife is what sex is, and that he had a right to her, to her emotions, to her body, to her intimacy, to her whole self and that she belonged to him completely, with no reason to see as why not.

The man I got married to thought that everything was good at face value, perhaps it never occurred to him that his wife could have been in love, perhaps he never saw when his wife wrote to him that how broken she was, perhaps he never saw that in those words what she was telling him is that she has lost love and now she is broken and not being able to come to terms, perhaps he never realized that she is trying to tell him that she is afraid of intimacy and yet, the man I got married to thought that he could bring in physical intimacy just by virtue of me being his wife, by forcing his wife to sleep with him.

I have had umpteen physical relationships in teenage and in college and in while working and I was berserk, starting from a point where I was curious about getting physical to being emotionally involved to getting depressed and getting physical, cos it gave me assurance to having a belief somewhere that I am in love with the person and sex was the purity in love to being liberal in having, sex, I developed a mind set where my body if someone desired did not matter, I gave it away, throwing it away, asking to take it as much and let me see how

much more can one take, here—take my body and let me see
how far can you go, here take it !

You b***t**d and I carried this pattern with the person, I got
married, here take my body, even if I hate it giving to you, here
take it, even I feel r***d by you, take and let me see how far the
animal in you can go.

However, in the process something changed. I understood
deep down, what am I looking in my life-partner, my
husband, what would he be like. He would be my husband,
my protector, someone who would be the last person to lay
his hands on me, someone who did not looked at my body
as skin and flesh, someone who will love my mind and soul
and give time to it, someone who would grow on my mind
and soul, someone who would give me shoulder to cry even
if other walked over me, someone who would not even touch
me until I am ready. someone who would heal my wounds,
someone who give me all the love that I lost, someone who
would be the soak when u cried at night, someone who would
weep with me, when I wept in lost love, someone who would
stay until I got out of my trauma, someone who would make
me pure, cos he was so pure and untouched perhaps, someone,
who see the life in me and of what I could be, not someone
who saw me what I was.

However, if I feel guilty about breaking this marriage, I feel
guilty and heart can never lie and I know it, cos everything in
between may have been incidental and reactional.

It leave me with thinking does it mean that I have to go back
to the man I got married, can I not say that yes I am guilty
and I feel deeply about it, however, I want to start my life

afresh and it does not mean going back to the same man, I got married on cards and paper. May be its time we forgive each other and start out lives afresh, for what has gone and happened in these years, cannot be undone, all we can do is understand each other and give permission to each other to live life, honestly and take it in our stride.

Hey what the heck the journey of life is not so long and so deep, it's a beautiful journey and one needs to drive through this with light heart and happily and with love. If love does not mean getting married to the man you, loved, it also does not mean, not to forgive in life and move on in life.

Love means forgiving and giving permission to live life of your own and to the lives of others. Love means having an open mind, love means welcoming life, love means having to get up once again, love means to allow you to be happy with you and love means to accept the way you are and others are. Love means to life higher and love to means look forward. And only one who loves oneself can one love others and love life!

IX. And history has more than what it offers

And says who, that history is only to find my roots, yes it is, history is to find out who I am and how did all people behave obnoxiously and its not only me.

Did history not tell us how love was lost and how desires were found by traveling far and wide, and how men traveled far and wide, cos he had lost his love that one emotion that made him so empty inside and so lonely inside that he took to the world and he marveled at what he did, at what he achieved, at what he pursued, cos he lost himself somewhere and in his pursuit he discovered the world, in his process to fill his own emptiness, he urged out, he went out, he went far and wide until he came to discover himself, until he conquered lands, until he conquered seas and oceans and when he was doing this blindly, there was one emotion that drove him through and through, either he was lonely deep inside and was only searching happiness and success and achievements to compensate and fulfill his deepest needs, and in the process history was being written.

When he lost his love, he took to his heart and found it broken, an emotion so strong and deep that he could not contain within and his outside manifestation was only the face of his healing up inside and thus the world came to know of this man, of his actions and somewhere he needed the whole world to correct itself to fill up his heart and heal himself.

For each and every action has an equal reaction. The world must have been have been discovered when the man lost himself and went out for search, a deep emotion within. The continents must have been conquered when the man needed to win his own heart and he took to the world. The civilizations were killed and vanished because that someone, who lead the war, was hurt somewhere deep inside. The nations were lead somewhere for freedom cos someone somewhere was dying to be free, to be free and feel that emotion, that nations were created and freedom was achieved.

History does not touch this, however I know when something good happens, it has an equally deep reasons pulling it through. Sometimes it changes the world, however I know when something like this happens, there is something very very deep personal experience attached with it. While some act on this and some do not.

My desire for riding is the healing inside me and extending it to take to millions of people. My desire for grape farming is to the lost sense in me of having my own children and thereby taking care of the plants to love them and give all what I have got. Its not that I am benevolent inside to teach riding or grow grapes to make millions of worth, however its my lost self, my healing, to find the lost me, to fill me up that I love to ride and grow grapes and take it further from there. In the world there is no philanthropy, it is only lost and found and that's what mostly drives the world.

That why when I read history, I find my reflection in that water, and I relate to myself better.

X.   I owe my Purpose on this earth to Allah

God has sent you with a purpose in life, on this earth
And my prime purpose is to fulfill this purpose
I owe my existence to fulfilling my purpose on this earth
And this is what I owe to Allah

The rest in life happens or are in our lives to fulfill this purpose in life. As incidents and happenings keep occurring in our lives, we are being driven closer to our purpose in life. As we keep coming across more and more people in our lives, they help us to become closer to our goals.

As we develop relationships in our lives, we keep getting closer to our purpose in life. Some relationships are life long. Also to fulfill our purpose in life, Allah has chosen our parents for us, our brothers and sisters and our friends, our life partners.

And as we progress in our lives and our purpose, there are, time-progressions which keep happening and keeps multiplying or which keeps diminishing from our lives. When we look at all the happenings from the outside, we label them as good or not so good; we label them as institutions or outside the institutions. We start judging them as correct or not correct. I learnt this, and it struck upon me, that I have a purpose in life and my prime focus in my life is to fulfill my living and my goal on earth. The people who I come across in my life make me realize my purpose more strongly, provided, I am listening to my heart.

If Zero is the scale of my purpose, there will be experiences on the left side and there will be experiences on the right side of zero, they will pull me on either side. Its just human society and years of discoveries and nomenclature that we call them as negative experiences or we call them as positive experience. However both make my Zero stronger and both experiences balances me and makes me stronger.

The people who I come in touch in my life, are here to lift me to my purpose, my being. They may come in form of my life partner, my soul mate, my mother, my father, my sister or my brother, my senior at work or my mentor in the race—course and many more. Hence my goal in life is not to find the person for me in my life, on the other hand my goal in life is to follow my purpose and all along, and people and relationship will keep coming to me. I also realize, as I become stronger in purpose, the kind of people I attract in my life. Its nerving to see this, cos I know behind all this is the Light of Allah leading me towards my purpose.

To follow my purpose is therefore my prime Aim and fulfillment. I as a part of human elements on earth, in Asia, in India, born in Nainital to my parents, my sister and my brother, having studied in different districts, and Ranchi and Delhi and working in Delhi and stumbling across what I thought was love and getting married and separated to someone I thought was my husband and staying far off in Mumbai, working in an automobile company, coming across few human being who I relate to and aspiring to be a Jockey Trainer and to do a formal education in horse education, is one of my milestones towards fulfilling my purpose.

And all what happened so far is not a coincidence. I see a proper plan in whatever happened and it was me only, sometime back, that I had labeled all, that happened to me. And now when I have a eagles view to the path of my life, and I start from where I came, I start looking the beginning I start seeing there is a greater purpose in my life and that I am not stopping myself for what I have come to for, on this Mother Earth. For I have a bigger purpose to Mother Earth and Father Human Evolution than my own parents. For I have a larger purpose to my Human brethren than my own brother and sister. For I have a larger purpose to my soul than to my physical being. For now I can see the puzzle coming a little in shape and I thank God for every thing, every human interactions that Allah provided to me, in realizing my Path.

XI. *What do you thrive on*

It's normal to be abnormal and it's okay if you face a lot of not so—positivity. As I got up this morning, I prayed to God, Oh, just one day, give me the strength to just move my today on my free will, for I knew that my mundane work at workplace will pull me through, its routine and its all decided about the workplace.

My life only starts after my workplace, for that's the place where my free will starts, for that's place, where I am the only master and I am only worker and I decide as to how it should go.

I decide if I am achieving something more than usual human being standing next to me in the local train rushing home possibly to meet their kids at home or parents at home, or may be just to be home or something, else. For when I stand by the local train and watch those eyes in the train, the eyes of young women, mother of two women, a not so young mother, older woman, I watch their eyes, and somehow I look into those eyes and I know what's their story is like. I look into their faces and I know, whether they had smiles in their lives, whether someone loved them in their lives, whether if had challenges in their life and how they met their challenges.

Challenges are part of life and they are integral for our growth, however I believe that its only how we meet these challenges, reflect our beauty of our faces, our shine of eyes, our sheen of skin, and our curve of smile we develop over all these period of time. Our faces tell so much about how we felt about the time which went by and the time that is now and the time that we look forward to.

The only thought that crosses my dual thinking mind is that I am not going to look like that woman, or this woman and it just enforces me to keep fighting up and meeting and blessing every challenge that I come across, its so nice, if one day does not pass by without throwing challenges actually means that we are not growing up or we did not learn any thing day.

For if the day passes like a passing cloud, and it not rest for a while, it did not grew up my life that day, like each drop makes an ocean, that day did not build me up, it just went by, just like that. So am glad that each is a challenge and some clouds stop by, to look into me. and I meet them with a smile, cos when I see these clouds, I deep down know that I am blessed and I am getting better and better each day.

And its when I knew that I thrive on disconnect and confusion, cos it helps me build my thoughts better and when I found that I thrive on madness and it is when I make sense out of things happening around me.

And I carry on, for I know that I looked back at the cloud and pushed it back to where it came from and here I take one more step closer to the world of my paradise and clear sky and green fields and flying birds and colorful flowers, my world of dreams in real.

XII. Dreamt such a vivid dream last night

Dreamt such a vivid dream last night, it was very real and happy and happening and everything was like a best thing that could happening in life . . . I remember a song being played and I was wearing a long skirt and long fur overcoat and then I took off my coat and I was doing the salsa steps on the tune and I felt so lovely about myself. It was just amazing.

There I was dancing with my partner and we were so graciously close to each other, my partner was holding me and we went round and round the whole wooden ground and we were together so gracious and in love. It was just like a breeze in the air flowing flawlessly and the bodies in perfect curve holding each other and the music flowing like the tradewinds over the desert, just taking off both of us from the ground and talking to air, in love with life.

And then we had to go somewhere and my partner was not very happy about going. I was there throughout and we were preparing beds for so many people, other friend's. My partner came and just lied down in his bed and was still and was calm and I was there next to him, holding every moment that I stood beside him. I knew in the heart of my heart that he did not want to go and he also could not say anything, cos my partner is not in habit of speaking anything that is not so positive, so there I was, however I my heart I was happy, cos I felt the same like my partner did and I was next to him, with him.

However, we decided to anyways enjoy life and we went ahead and then was in the midst of people and good music and I wanted to dance and I did and took off my overcoat and I danced like a lady and like a wave in the ocean and like a breeze in the mountains and like a sand in the dunes and like a music in the guitar, like a free hand drawing in the canvas, like a falling snow in the mountains, like a flying drape in the air, like the falling shine in the moonlight, like the starts smiling in the sky.

And this was the lovely dream that I ever dreamt in my dreams, so vivid, so live!!

XIII.   Celebration of my being

My life is an absolute celebration of my being. For I love myself the way I carry and the way I look at life. For I celebrate every moment that I live and I learn from it. My endeavor to reach my fullest potential what God created me to be allows me to live every moment and relish the experience that I live through it.

For now when I look at my life I enjoy every moment thinking about the path I traveled and the path I am creating for myself and the path where I am on right now. Cos every thing and the way I feel about everything in life is accepting and being thankful to God, for every experience, He grants me and leads me to. I am sure that every thing I go through only leads me to my purpose and closer to my goal in life, therefore to say anything and qualifying anything is absolutely non essential, cos it is only when I walk, live through every moment in life do I become the person that God has endeavored me to become.

And today I am a more open person that I used to be, today I am more receptive about life, cos when I open to all the possibilities in life and life will open to me for all that is stored in life.

So when I stand here today and look where I came from and lived on my own, I feel proud of myself when I tried everything for the first time in my life and I did that. I dared to take action and that's the respect of my being. I ran when I was having my periods and stood a winner in the race.

I brunt mid night oil in the summers of 45 degrees of temperature and with a towel underneath my hand, I practiced the mathematics sums, so that the note book I was writing on, does not get wet.

I liked someone, this was a true admiring someone at the level where you want to get in life and I met that someone. It was a good moment. I tried that first beer and it's a different thing, I didn't like it. Yet, I dared and I did it. For I knew that it was something that was not liked by people from my end. However it is different fact that I liked the old monk in the black with coke and continued for quite sometime. Until it was time to say good bye to the Old Monk.

I loved riding the horses and it gave a great belief and a sense of my being. It brought me closer to nature. I clicked and loved the way I do it, still. Now I endeavor to sing the classical sing and dance the classical dance.

I endeavor to grow the plant and plant the seeds of nature and take care and be a mother to nature. Cos I am a mother and that's what God made a woman for, a mother, to care, to love, to bear, to carry, to deliver, to feed and to grow and now I endeavor all that and thus I celebrate my being on this earth.

When I cut my hair very small and they start growing, I like them; I love them, cos it's their freedom time. I allow them, my life long partners in me to be what they are. my hair, my eyes, my skin, my toes, my nails, my body, my back, my shoulders, I just love them the way they are, cos when they are themselves, they give back the best to me, and brings out the best. And I celebrate their being. And in turn they celebrate my being.

And, I think, that

Celebration of being is a prayer
Celebration of being is love
Celebration of being is happiness
Celebration of being is to care
Celebration of being is self respect
Celebration of being is spreading happiness
Celebration of being is to live life completely
Celebration of being is allowing
Celebration of being is accepting
Celebration of being is learning
Celebration of being is worship
Celebrating of being is spiritual
Celebration of being is a celebration in itself
Cos it brings the highest form in human being
Cos it brings out the best in me

XIV. Companion in my Journey

☺No, I am not looking at my past, I am looking at how to better my future and live my present. when I come home and open my door, the unlocking of the lock and key and that latch, I am unlocking the happiness of my home and when I step in, I am absorbing the wealth of happiness and the filling up of the waiting-ness of my home at home. my plants I long to touch them, to wash them, to love them and to talk to them, my plant in the pot, who spreads its arms and each day it keeps getting, day by day and I smile looking the growth of plant, of a living being in my own home, which is an extension of His creation.

And sometimes, I slide into the love of myself and love of my own life and creation, cos basically I think I am like a horse, who loves to graze and be on the open green fields in the sun and green grassland and love to graze and rest and enjoy its freedom, and its only when the horse senses any danger, does the horse runs and when it runs, it becomes wild and then, no one can touch it, cos it is running for its life, else horse is very gregarious animals, loves company and loves peace in life.

And that's how sometimes, when I step into my den, my cave, my home sweet, home, I become a different person, I am mother to myself, I am mother to my feet, I am love to my heart, I am sweetheart to my body, I am the lover of my face and skin, I am the darling of my legs which long to rest and I am the companion of my mind, I am the sister of my hunger and my health, for then I set out to love myself the way I am, the way, my skin is.

I take care of my body, my mind, I read and put lovely thoughts in my mind, that sometimes I cry out on excitement for how beautiful can a thought be, more than this, I admire me, I thank me for carrying myself for a lovely day, I love myself for not giving up at the moment when things seemed so dark and down, I say hats off to my attitude to carry on and then I set out to have little feast with myself, everyday, I set out to the jungle of world and I return to my den everyday at night.

During the day I look forward to move around with full heart and soul around this jungle and creation in it and sometimes I think I am digging gold, cos I take with me what I like and leave what I do not and in the process, sometimes in the process I touch upon others peoples life and it makes me happy.

Times when I contemplate for the kind of rules and structures we, the mankind has made on this earth and for running the economy, for I know that its time that a quite revolution is taking place and the economy will takes its turn, for its been more then 50 years that our economy is due to change, although so much has changed in just last 10 years that I feel that ten years before was another age.

However the more this age is setting its pace for change, the more is the increase of the need for the human being to go back its original shape, thereby meaning the peace of jungle, the chant of Om, the reading of shlokas, the playing of sports put in the open fields, the singing of songs in the classical way, cos it has a science in it for human health body mind and soul, cos the speed at which human being is progressing could also indicate the pace at which it will sweep off, cos the changes today is creating much imbalance and therefore the human relations with God and self is getting shortened.

And we see the little signs of rehabilitation here and there today, with practice of Yoga and gaining the importance in today's life, the going to the nature, the increase awareness of spiritualism.

Infact, sometimes from my own, life, I see myself becoming closer to God, with the events progress in my own life. when I conflict of values, or any feeling that I need to overcome, or even if it is a transaction related to money or people, I become closer to God, cos I find strength in that, and I am sure that most human beings are moving onwards this, cos I feel that human being is becoming more lonely than before and the only salvation if being closer to God and therefore, Self and thus reclaiming life.

And it is in this time that I like revisiting the events of the past of thousands of years back, cos I believe that its more or less a circle, means, like the seasons come in cycles, so will the civilizations will, there patterns will, may be when we visit our history, we ca learn something and become more aware of ourselves, cos today is nothings but the cause of what we did yesterday, however the present is the choice we have in our hands to exercise and thus make our future.

Choice is such a lovely concept and a such a practical and integral part of life, for if the choice was not there, we would not have been able to design our life's, our cities, our countries our civilizations, we all are, what we are, cos of the choices we as a human being made in our lives, in our homes, in our cities, in our countries and as a civilizations on this earth.

I drift in my thoughts starting form one point to another and sometime I think it's only in this age we can afford to think too much, I am sure our ancestors 1000 years back did not have to think so much, to take action at that point of time.

And may be that's why the exercising of choices today is very important, by saying this I, in no way mean that it was not important during that age, however I may want to convey that we must have made macro choices during that time, today we have micro and macro choices and thus drifting of thoughts is what I see a natural.

However now coming back, as I step into my home, at makes me happy that I spend considerable time with myself and my thought and where I am going on this life path, spending time to see the moon and the stars and the sun going up in the morning for it is during those moments I live my life and I propel myself to move forward in life.

The beauty of today that I think each human has become entity like the flying in protons and is capable of getting out of the orbit or reaming in the orbit and the beauty is still to keep rotating, and not loosing one identity in the path. And I am glad that I live myself fully on this path and am living fully, self propelling myself, for what others think of my life does not make any difference to me and in my way of living and I am glad that I have been able to overcome the way other determined my life, than the way, I determine my life today and I quite like it. I salute to my attitude who has always kept with me, in all the times and my mind who has always been my twin soul and my heart, who has so alive and pumping the life in me and carrying me on this path and each and every part of me who are my companion on this journey.

XV. *Energies coming together—Synergy*

I think life is all about the synergies coming together, and its when the right energies meet and come together, there is a positive movement and its when the energies are out of order, do we have, not so positive movement and that's what human being has named as overcoming or struggle or challenges and otherwise it is called simple and flowing and natural, cos by the end of it, the energies which are traveling in space are, all there and are looking for the right counterpart to travel together and when this happens there is a spurt of energy in the space and we feel it very strongly within ourselves and outside us and it is when the environment also gets effected, it makes one feel light and balanced and gives a feeling of ecstasy and peace at same time.

Sometimes I think that whatever path, I travel in my life and whatever I experience in my life is meant to be there, cos it is preparing me to meet what is meant to be mine for me in my life and I am getting prepared for it, min by min, hour by hour and day by day. So whatever is happening in life is great and I welcome and I thank God for the same.

And whoever said that one needs to settle only one time, I will settle hundred times until I meet my soul mate and I will know and I will get prepared in the process, its not about breaking up or leaving the relationship, its about getting prepared for the final one, its about the people who came to my life all these years, owed me and I owed them and when we are through we moved on, it was only that time that we had to stay together, and its true for both sides, not just one side.

My religion is when I am not happy and something brings tears to me eyes, means its not good for me and I move on and when something that gives happiness to my heart and makes me good about myself is good for me and is something I will look forward to repeat this experience in life, it could be for few times and it could be forever. And that's my religion.

XVI. *Nature brings in the peace in me*

And as I sit in the window, to look outside and look into my future, stepping out from where I got run into in my life, I look forward to my life, to my future, to my twins, to my glory, to my shine, to my purpose in life, to be me, for what God made me to be.

While I sit here and I know that the moment of release is yet to come and I know, that this ride may not be smooth, for I will have to overcome somethings and will have to learn to accept few things, for the better for each and for better peace of mind, I will have to look at the bigger picture, I sit here today, I pray to God to give peace of mind to both minds and help both minds to come out of this gracefully and start new life for each one of us afresh and step closer to our purpose in life.

I pray that God give strength to both mind and leave with a feeling lighter and better and looking forward to life and have the best in lives respectively. For I believe that whatever happens is for the Good and challenges that we have in out lives is to make ourselves better human being, what God desired human being to be.

For may be our lives were only for this interception, and I am sure will leave each one of better of.

However, one has to go through the process to reach the end results. I am not looking at getting stuck in the process and only looking at the end results. Still, one has to go through the process, cos I believe it's the process which shapes a human mind, helps him to overcome weakness and achieve patience in life and he becomes and changes from within and that helps him to go further in life and progress in life and purpose.

And while I sit here containing myself within, I look outside the window, I look at the flock of birds and leafs that shine from trees and the grass ground and the purple flower that hang down from the tree and the pigeons playing on the field, it somewhere touches my soul and reaches the nature within me, to be one with me and I feel one with nature and thus I become one with time and my patience grows in me.

And must I say that it is strange however such is the time when our learning and what we talk about and share with other people actually comes in test, cos this is the time, when we are on real test on what we believe, think positive, take initiative, think and plan affirmations, trust and have faith in God, believe and just do the deed and rest is taken care by God, honestly, its all this that I am sitting here and thinking and I realize if I am not practicing all this, then, what did I learn, cos now is the time that I implement all this, to enable me to forge ahead and take care of myself like a little girl, who is with her mother and is being taken care of and help close to her loved one, cos the little girl knows that her mother will take care of her and nothing in world is stronger than the mothers love and that's how I feel, the little child in me is like a child and I am the mother to this lovely child of mine, cos I love her and I will allow her to evolved her through this process.

And that's when this writing is also coming in handy to me, cos writing helps me take out the expressions in me and feel at level and feel stable and good and when my heart is poured out, I fill it with my love for myself and that's how I take control of the moment of time. For, I know that each moment in life, I embrace it with love and I trust it will make a lovely human being and thus turn everything around me is loving and beautiful.

And while I sit here and type this, I hear the azaan. It's very powerful I think, it gives me strength and gives me peace and reminds me of Allah all the time, that He is near me and by my side and that I am the blessed child of His.

Allah 'O Akbar!

XVII. De-Married

After the first stage is done, now is it a matter of time, compulsory time that one has to go through and I am sure that I do not see any reason as why this should not get through.

In fact, now is the time that I am setting my life more carefully, designing it more carefully, cos I do not know however I have a feeling that now I need to carry myself more gracefully, and working towards what I had always dreamt in life. for I can see that life is throwing one possibilities after the other on myself and now is the time that I embrace life completely and run with it, for now is the time that I choose the ball and run with it, for now is the time that I start ticking off the checklist of dreams that I have written down.

The flip side of divorce is that one is no more married, rather one is de-married, means that one stills looks forward to getting married and having a family and children and it's but natural. The other flip side is also, although, while in separation, one is not staying together, however, there is a feeling that one is married and hence the steps of life are very careful in anything one does and it becomes a way of life. the feeling of marriage may not come from staying together, but just by the simple fact that one is married, the simple fact that one has taken those rounds around the fire and has gone through that function, I cannot imagine how much does this function effect ones mind, ones mind may not be attached to the person when one is getting married or had got married, however there is sure a feeling that it leaves behind and that is one feeling with which one grows up into a adult and no more is a single.

The flip side of having getting divorced is that one is again on its own, however, this kind being on ones own, is different and sure, one may be tempted towards some kind of relationship. The only thing I am conscious of is that I do not get into the path of some vacuum of a vacuum, you know, when one stays separate in a marriage, there is a vacuum that comes in life, even if one was married only for 15 days and separated for another 4 years, now when one gets completely divorced, suddenly this vacuum goes and there is a vacuum of a vacuum. However, I believe that, being clear one ones purpose, one cannot go haywire cos it is the purpose, which keeps the human mind on the path.

Its strange, however, I am over with the sexual desires anymore, I am through with them and it does not excite me anymore, the only thing which I look forward to, is having my own twins girl twins and taking care of them and living each and every dream of mine while on this earth.

Being a single before marriage and after marriage is like the lights coming up in the room during the day, young and light and no one not even realize its intensity and after is like the light in the night, when the day has gone and night has set in and the moon is little relaxing and towards ending the day and one goes through ones day to sleep finally.

There is one more thing I realize, one does not fight against any odds, however when is clear one ones purpose, one just walks past to reach that path, so one is not fighting against any odds, it's the same person, however his or her purpose has just become clear, when one runs with that purpose in mind and heart, its just that one does not see the obstacles on the way, one just brushes away the thorny bushes to make way for the garden of ones purpose, ones dream. To the world, it may look like ones purpose, however, to one self, it is not so, it's very simple.

XVIII.   Off My Chest

I am glad that I have off led this load from my chest in telling Dad, that I have gone ahead with my divorce case and that it bothered me to tell home, cos I was thinking, as to how would he react to this. Now it is not so important, in life that what I do in my life, in my life after this, cos I know deep down what I am looking for, however papa will have to accept this fact that I have my own life and I am allowed to live my life as how I want and love to, and in this process, I do not look for his approval of my life and I live my life as per my wishes and as what I want to. I have full responsibility as how I want to. And I love this situation, cos from now, on, I am on my own and do not have to live as per others wish me to live and have a responsibility and accountability to myself and this is the one of the biggest step. Towards my freedom and my choice in life and I am happy that I took this decision in my life

XIX. And Yet again all about Love and Loving

And yet again, the nature in me back again. It feels so good; to get up in the morning and watch the sky, with scattered clouds and its just looks beautiful. And breathtaking and lo my camera, cos how can I not honor the morning and capture it in my camera with me, always.

And yet again, the tune of music stirs my feet and hands and arms and body and yet again, I get up from my bed to sway on the music again to reach the state of high, irrespective of place, person and thing, I dance and dance like a wave on the ocean and wind in the sky and flowers in the sea beach and I feel the same in my hands flowing and my feet waving and my body in rhythm and my arms flowing like the flowers in the midst of valley when the breeze touches them.

And yet again my fingers itch to write and when words flow out from my fingers, I know that it is best self and my state of being. and I just thought that no matter how I do it and for how long I do what, if I keep doing the things I love to do, I will run into that one thing which I will just pick up and run with in life, life is about doing the things what one loves to do, it could be for short period of time or it could be forever, for you and I may not know if this for life, or was it for only that period of life and it is suppose to be give and leave what is needed in that period of time only when one needs it the most, cos the thing, that we love to do, is something our heart desires to do and in kept in heart for a long time and one needs to release it into the air, to become free and give freedom to that one thing which one loves to and that's why we feel light when we do the things that we love to do.

Its about freeing the self and the soul and freedom, to sway in the air and rest upon to where it belongs to. If the thing belongs to self, it will rest on self and if, it does not, it will find its home, to blossom. I believe in doing what one loves to and there is no concept of sacrifice or even maintaining the discipline, cos discipline in the manifestation of inner heart, cos when inner heart and mind and body and soul in sync with each other in its purpose, when one discovers it, the rest of the senses and body parts falls in place to align the purpose of all senses and this is attainting freedom of self and mind and soul.

O mankind therefore, stop not from doing the things you love to do, it may be anything. And there is nothing as good or bad or any degrees to anything. it is all relative and seeing from where one is standing and do not worry if you have hurt someone in the process with all your sincere heart and mind, for if it hurts someone, means the other person 's mind is not strong enough to accept it, or the other person is looking or taking things in a very very relative matter and so be it anything which come from heart and mind in the purest form will not and cannot harm anyone, hurt anyone and time fills in all the gap to soothe anything.

For if all of us start living the life which our inner voice tells us, then each one of us will be a happier soul on this earth. the hurt and hatred and failures will disappear from this earth and world will be a better place to live and we will become more and more sensitive to each other and respect and love and peace will flow and prevail.

For if each one of us will do the things that we love to do, there will be more harmony in the world, cos each one of us is born with a life inside and this life needs to be released out in the open for it to come to its best and fullest form.

And what if instead of using the money as the exchange, starts exchanging in goods, it would so much better, for we will then be more sensitive to what we need and what prices we will have to pay in order to receive, what our heart and mind desires and life would be a better place and relationships would be based on interchange and interdependence and right people coming in touch with each other based on the mutual interest and with this will come the relationship aspect and respect too. The mind will evolve and will become more receptive for give and take. And give and take is all what is life is about.

God gives us life to live on this earth and we take it gracefully, for fulfilling our purpose for which we are on earth. For us we take life and give back ourselves to life and in between we keep completing the smaller gives and take to make the bigger Give & Take to happen, in the long run.

And to this achieve Balance in nature, in the water, in the air and in the land and enhancing the life of mother nature, and keeping it young, for if the balance in nature is continued and there is no disharmony anywhere, the aberrations will not appear and thus it will not effect either us or the place, this nature where we live and celebrate our living, each day and each hour, each min and each second.

For if the thoughts we think are in line with what we feel, there will be no dis-balance and dis-ease and imagine this by thousands and thousands of each living soul on this earth, I can almost see a rhythm in the wave, if each one of are in sync with our feelings and this earth would be then, just a wave dancing along together beautifully.

For it's in nature, when the bird flies along with the wind, the flight is most beautiful and effortless and in the direction of which the bird wants to fly. For if the waves rhythm with the flow of the water, ocean is at its most peace and at its most beauty, for if the trees sways along with the direction of breeze, it life is longer and it almost appears like the dancing of the nature and happiness prevails.

For do not feel guilty or get bogged down, when you are happy with smaller things deep inside or smile or see that there does not seem to be many many challenges in life, for God did not create me, to struggle in life, but love and be happy in a very seamless manner in the direction of my purpose. and for if there is too much of struggle of effort, listen to your body, your mind and soul, to listen to what are saying or feeling about the larger direction in life and you will know. For a man is not born to go through pain and misery and fight in life, but man is born to be happy in his life and spread happiness around and make this world a better place, for a man who is struggling himself, how will he be, the messenger of love and happiness?

So I am here to enjoy my life every min and love myself every minute and as life will go on, I will blossom into a beautiful person that God desired me to be.

XX. Being on the Driver's Seat

And often I wonder and think and talk to myself about how I grew up and studied, only cos that was the only thing which gave me back the praises and recognition, so studies and marks were only the tool to get back some attention and praises in life from my significant ones and it became the order of the day.

And how I grew up to live my freedom out in the open of the hostel, to breathe that fresh air, that walk in the woods and that sitting by the side of river and my vehicle was that college where by default I was become an engineer by qualification. My only goal was that of freedom, that girl like the Alice in wonderland, who wanted to wild and free and with nature and with herself, my urge to be with myself goes a little too far, but then I think if it is my urge, it is my urge and why should I fight against it.

From that land of rivers and woods to the land of concrete jungle to live on my own, to cook my own supper, to let my demons come out in open and let myself free, I made myself light again, cos it all had to get out of my system and it got out and it found its way and it was out of my mind, body and soul cos now when I look back I feel good about myself and I never ever see any acts as labeled as good or bad, but I see all that as so much important in me, cos I was carrying, may be carrying all that in my heart and in my mind and I freed myself of those thoughts and became clean in the process, for I see the whole life as a purification process and in this process we go through something in life which our intelligence tells us to judge it as good and bad, however on the larger meaning of this is that we are freeing ourselves of the thoughts which our body cannot contain and our minds get stifled of and then go on to the path, where, our minds finds peace and balance in.

From the city of fast cars and concrete jungles, my mind retaliated and yet again, found the place, where I was close to nature again, where I could breathe the fresh air and take walk in the jungle, old jungle, see the peacock dancing and rain smelling and life was at peace again, until I landed in the city of dreams, a city which taught me to live and fight back and be on track for what I love to do and would do. the city took me in its lap and carried my like a baby, showed me its arms of nature, where I could crawl upon and be myself, the city which gave me a warm hug and a cool presence of itself by the way of its rains and the sea water and waves, where I could slip down to my basic self and where I could start learn to crawl and walk a little in life and at every fall the city took my in its arms and cradled me to the mother nature and taught me that its okay to fall in life and its okay to pursue to do things which I deep down always wanted to do. The city cleansed me and touched my soul, cos before that I was removing the layers that that covered my soul and my body and my mind and I was getting exposed to just nature and myself with the only nature in between to enhance the beauty of my mind and my imagination and my self.

Working in a towers was again a vehicle to add fuel to my nature walks, to add wind to my trot, to add cushion to my writings, to extend my imagination and how I love to see and capture the world, the way I see it. And there it brought me to stage, where once in while learning to walk and then run, I would fall and walk and run again and would allow myself to get lost in the rhythm on the music and that search in the gullies and that touch of the animal and that listening of the raindrops and that singing from the vocal cord. Life allowed me to venture into my being, into the purpose of my living.

Rest all is by default, for the college and the capital city working and the studies again and then the work again, is only by default and is not a destination, but only a journey. for corporate life is not a destination and becoming a VP is not a destination, but only a journey, coming to work and Buildings is not a destination and an end in itself, but its journey and the journey to become the best that God created, the journey, like thousands of other human beings are in the journey, to touch their lives and enhance their journey, to get few of them on track, who have become off track and out the in motion and hence reaching a balance.

And once the purpose becomes clear the milestones and the journey becomes simpler to follow and to lead and get lead in this journey. And its not a surprise that sometime while on this journey we forget that the milestones is itself a destination and there is not further to go, however when I keep myself close to nature, it helps me to realize that vehicles and milestones are only the symbol of how far have I come and how far do I have to go and only a parameter of how my journey was and to make any alterations in my journey further on this highway, on this road, through the jungles of people, through the desert of pushing ahead, through the waters of uncertainty, through the air of mixed feelings at times and through the spirit of moving ahead and becoming one with my purpose.

Through this Journey, I touch upon many things that seem to be lovely and touching my heart, however, when the heart is fulfilled, I know that its time to proceed, to which an outside world may mistake for leaving it half way, for nothing is half way, it has a beginning and it has and end and only our heart knows when it started and when it ended, however the outside manifestations could be very very misleading. So I go by my heart for I am the only window to my own heart and own mind and I would know it the best and my conscious would never ever betray me for it's my inner voice, it's the voice of God within me.

Hence,

What may appear to be abrupt may be an end and beginning of something real and good

What may appear to be unsound may be actually the soundest of everything I did

What may appear to be ugly may be the beginning of something that's beautiful

What may appear to be weak to outside may the most strongest of act from within

What may appear to be so called bad may be the beginning of liberating one self and path to freedom & cleansing

What may appear to be in shortage may actually the beginning of what is started to grow from within

What may appear to be a failure, may be the only start of the road to success

So stay close to heart and not the world

Stay close to conscious and not the voices outside

Stay close to the self and not to the faces outside

For the journey that I endeavor, where I am headed is only I know

Other only see me, from their window of the vehicle of their journey

And their vision is always from their angle of the front or rear mirror, its not as it is

The journey that I am headed on, is the path that I only see from my seat

And nobody could be driving the same vehicle on the same seat at one time

So go on and drive and keep the eyes on the vision, which only you can see!

XXI.   Letter to my love, my life

Dear Anita,

I know sometimes you go through the phases where in you think too much about the future, and you know that it affects you in not such a good way. You invariably get cold and I have noticed that when you are thinking too much about the tomorrow, it does gets into your system, so you know what the one thing you will have to take from me with all my heart is that I love you and I am always with you and will never ever let you down in life, so always when you think you feel alone and think too much about the future, always remember that I will always come around and take care of you, dear. and in my hands you are safe like a child, for remember that you are more than a child to me, you are my own part, you are my breathe and heart beat and everything you do effects me in the similar way as it does to you, for remember if you even feel a little low, I feel in doubly and ten times more, cos I cannot see you in pain ever, my girl.

So, in such time, just hold my Hands and you will feel the warmth from me, soothing you down, you will feel me hugging you with my big arms and you can put your head on my shoulders and you will sleep like a child in my arms, until I put you to bed and I come around and watch you sleep like an angel.

Never let that tear drop from eyes, for your tears are like pearls to me, save them and drop them for when you are happy and they will flow like pearls and then you are going to have so much happiness and blessings in your life that you will then run out of these pearls in your eyes, they bring the twinkle in your eyes.

And always remember that I have full faith and trust in you and I am proud of you, for what you are and for not what you do, cos that is a different thing what you do, for I know, cos the person that you are, whatever you will do, will be of the same degree, so I do not have to worry about what you do, cos you are a beautiful person and only blossom, You are a blessed child and a happy child of God and I am the messenger of God to you, closest to you. God has sent me to protect you and blossom you while you live this life on earth.

So dear, I will be there to hold if you fall,
I will be there to lift you if you slip on the way
I will be there to guide you, if you lose your way
I will be there to wash away your tears, if you ever cry
I will be there to jump and cheer for you, when you succeed
I will there to hold your hand when you need one
I will there to hug you when you need it the most
I will be there to kiss you good night, each night you sleep
into world of dreams
I will be there to listen to you, when you have something
to say
I will there to caress you when you need it the most
I will be there for you every step; with every single step you
walk I will walk two
With you, I am
And love you, like I love myself.

Love & Courage
Yours only,
Anita

XXII.   Unheld, Free and Flowing

As I sat near the ocean today, I saw the big huge sun meeting the periphery of the earth. The sun was the most amazing circle I ever saw or could ever think that I could draw—huge round, big, smiling, red and orange color; I do not know who the two colors meshed like one soul with each other. It had a dash of clouds in between, the grey and dark grey dash of colors running through making and dividing it into two to the world who were watching the same, however, one could not deny the roundity of the sun. I saw the earth coming up, moving up and therefore the sun becoming smaller and smaller and portions of the sun covered by the large size of earth, on the other side of which, I was sitting.

The ocean water was slow today and it took effort for the waves to rise and fall against the rock and as the waves rose and fell, there was an effort in rising and thudding against the rock bed. The other extreme end of the ocean was getting itself drawn into a darker and darker line of periphery, so today, had I been that far, at that outer ring of the ocean, perhaps, I would be in a little more of the dark, that in the circle, I was sitting.

The earth spinned a little more and I saw the earth covering the sun more and more and until I saw the last arc of the sun and the earth becoming one and lo, in terms of the human being the sun had set, I was thinking, had the sun set ? or did the earth move on, on its course and I was farther away from the sun, until tomorrow morning I will see the sun again when earth had moved enough and closer to the sun and I would see the earth moving out as against in evening I saw the earth moving in now, today.

The sun having set in traditional accepted terms, I saw the water of the sea, a little more turbulent and free and now the movement of the water was more natural. More romantic and more energy came in. I saw the under currents from very far off, becoming stronger and stronger as they came in near the shore and I saw that the movement, was passed on from water to water, from waves to waves, until in the end, the movement became so strong that a big, large, long white wave was created and it could not contain itself and got transformed into a wave like a running horse's mane, the waves falling happily into the bed of rocks near the shore.

The waves were now running into all together, holding hands, holding arms, for each other and moving seamlessly into one another and breaking on together, splashing, holding, dancing, talking, jumping, smiling, making love with each other, it seemed.

I was listening to the waves and watching them, reflecting my thoughts, I was trying to listen to my thoughts and it seemed that my tears would flow to join those waves, along with them, holding hands, holding arms, moving together, becoming one and rising to the, fall, on the bed of rocks.

I wish I could just let my tears flow and become one with the waves, not because I was sad or was hurt, but because, I could not contain the freedom of the waves and together, the water in my attracted the waves and I sitting there was sure a waterfall myself, the waterfall of my tears running and catching with the waves in the ocean, going deep very deep and out back into the open ocean, along with other waves, free and together into the unknown world, changing moods, becoming still and rippling and rising and falling and basking in the sun and dancing in the moonlight and starlight, to become its most beautiful and yet unheld and flowing forever.

XXIII. Sitting on my window

Sitting on my window, this eve, I feel loved by the field outside, down below my window, which has a green grass with patched of wet mud and dry mud meshing through the grass laid out like the bed on the earth with rows of trees and little mounts where some floral shrubs flower out to the open sky mingling their fragrance to flow into the air that's dancing silently. The poles of lights all across the garden seem to be talking to each other as if holding the glances across to meet their bright shiny eyes, to look into Each others eyes to fall in love with their being and existence and as how impatiently they waited for the sun shine to hide and light up in the night to dance and meet and greet each.

The branches of the trees over hung to see what's in the ground in such a darkness, to find out down in the ground and to lower their ears of leaves to listen as if what's the ground talking to them in this soothing evening, with no more of scorching heat of the day. It looks as if the branches have lowered themselves to feel their own swing in the coolness of the moon and the air and that finally they are resting from holding themselves up during the day.

It looks like the planes going from above in the sky have only come to spot, light the ground, to give that special effect of the nature stage, to salute to the greenery and the grass and the earthy mud and little earthy mounts, making it look so very special and giving it just enough light from the top to make it feel special and yet not make it shy of its beauty.

The playing swings stand in the ground, so still and so serene that when one looks at it, it seems as if they have gone to sleep, tired of children jumping on them since long in the morning and now they rest and find peace in that silence, to slip into the night and become the holding tray of the mist falling in the night, to bathe themselves in the drops of moisture soothing their steel and steely stands that holds them.

The sound of prayers fulfilling the ground with the air that this beautiful nature is Gods creation and echoes into the heart of the ground, absorbing each note of the sound rising and falling into the bosom of the ground like the seamless flow of the music on the waves of the ocean.

And myself watching all this from my window, from the top, feel as if I am flying over the earth's most lovely creation, and that my love is flowing down to touch the ground, to feel the earth down, below, from my eyes, to listen to that sound of prayers, to view that hanging of the trees, to see the poles of lights celebrating the moment.

Besides me, from my window, I almost see that the ground, on the outer ring and periphery is surrounded with the mountains with tiny lights glowing from their arms, some lights rowed and some dotted in its own way, big lights and small lights, round lights and square lights, overlooking and surrounding the ground to protect it from the outside world, to posses the beauty inside the ground, to guard and to hold it for long.

Sitting on my window, how much I think that every little thing, object has life in itself. Is it not in the power of us to give life to everything that we see and observe and that how much everything symbolizes life, living and being and passing away? For everything that 'is ', breathes and speaks and conveys and tells and absorbs and has its own beauty. Did someone say it so true that "beauty lies in the eyes of the beholder" for someone who's mind is beautiful is pretty and fulfilling.

Its that thread of thought that gives life to everything on this earth, on and beyond this earth, so much that the stone, the flowers, the steel, the earth, the grass, the flying planes, the surrounding mountains, the bright lights on the tip of the steely poles, all seem to carrying a message for life and living and breathing in such a way that to me everything seems to beyond being life and being lifeless.

May be as I grew up and observed and saw and gathered, I find life in everything around me, some seeming to speak up and some so silent that it conveys so much more without saying or being able to speak, but by responding to everything that surrounds it and embraces it, like the stone on the ground lying there and still having the history and once, much lived life and holding that life inside it, present zillions of years back and holding so much inside.

Sitting on my window as I see this, I am overwhelmed by the creation and the one Who created!

XXIV. My journey to being back to Virgin

And it happened on its own. And I did not foresee it and neither did I think it would be so seamless and simple. I was infact very finicky and shaky about being and independent and being on my own self, cos in a way it meant complete freedom and totally free for doing anything that I want, anytime that I want and anywhere that I want and I discovered, once left so free, so amazingly free in coordinate of space and time and self, I found that true myself, so engulfed in just searching something within, searching through my readings, my books, my writings, my nature, my paintings, my own self that no one and no one on the outside interested me at all, it was like, I am flying high over the ocean and looking for something in the ocean, floating and that nothing interests me, neither the boat, nor the yatch, nor the ship, neither the dolphin, nor the motor boat, its just that I am flying and that's it and I cant see anything else.

Such is my journey to being back to my self, my original self. I feel as if I was once swimming in deep waters, in deep oceans, and eating the fish and playing with the dolphins, and was running after the colorful motor boats. Its something like, once I was the flower myself, attracting the bee and bee sucking the honey in me and then I would rest for a while, sway with the wind, bask in the sun shine and wet myself in the rains and I will bloom again to attract the bee when I am ripe and full.

However, now I am not in that ocean anymore, I am flying above that ground, I can see everything but it does not interest me anymore, I fly pursuing the sun in the noon and the moon and stars in the night, thinking that its my destination, cos every morning when I take a flight when the sun rises, it seems so near, I almost fall in love with it and I fly towards it and in eve when the moon comes high in the sky and stars abound, it seems like sun took the shape and color of moon and I fly again to meet it, cos the sun and moon are my new love and the deep waters does not interest me anymore, the dancing dolphins do not distract me anymore.

This is my journey towards becoming untouched and pure, cos in my pursuit of becoming closer to moon and the sun and the stars, I distance me from the deep waters, from the colorful motor boats, from the yatches, from the flying fishes and stars bees.

And it is then, I do not even feel or does not arise the need of wanting to step down to the waters, and touching the seas and the oceans and the hood of the boat or the oars of the boat, or the flag and robe of the yatch or the handle of the ship.

And therefore in the process I become the virgin again, untouched. And I know that while I fly high in pursuit of my love, I am being seen by the deep waters, and the dancing dolphins and I am quite liked and adored by when seen from down below, however I am not touched too, when I am flying so high for it takes effort and when done would not be possible as one would land down with a thud and there, therefore I am in a parallel universe in my own pursuit, becoming untouched and sacred and pure.

For who knows that there will a wave so high which will embrace me and engulf me and my flight and will tossle and turn with me, with the same intensity that I am flying high with and would subtly prick the virginity of my thoughts, my flight, my self, my sensuality and my being.

May be that wave will come, and until then, I continue to fly high, not noticing what is in deep waters and deep seas and colorful masts and honking ships. For once in a while my mind does go to the twinkling waters in the ocean and the shining and shimmering waves when still, however, so far have I come and so far, am I flying from the ground that now it seems like a heavy landing to touch that shimmering waters, to feel that coolness of the ocean, to dance and toss with the high waves, to kiss and play with the dolphins, so far have I come that now it seems a little difficult to come down and break my journey of flight that I am pursuing of.

May be it will take the big wave to rise to me, when I am flying a little lower in my own pursuit, may be during the sun set or during the sun rise, when I am a little lowered down and comes, this wave, to take me, to break me and hold me, to touch me, to splash me with the deep waters cooling myself and engulfing me around, to toss and to turn, to play and to rhythm, to follow and to run, to cover and to be covered, to become one.

But until then, I am the virgin yet again.

XXV. *What is it with you*

What is it with you. Sometime when I just live moment to moment, I feel as if I am complete, however when I see little far away, it seems not clear, why is that so. Does it mean that the future is not captured in the moment that we live or what it is. Sometimes I just feel like celebrating the moment, with my flowing gown, with my dancing shoes with heels, with my hair flowing, with my robes flowing, in a huge high ceiling hall with music talking to air and me dancing with hand in hand, close very close and held like the flower held by hand, like the airplane flowing in the sky, like the light held in the room, like the fragrance held in the air, like the leaves of tree held by its branches, like the birds held in the nest, like the eyelids by the eyes, like the reins held by the jockey on the horse, like the robes held by the shapely body, like the love held in ones hands, like the warmth held in ones heart and I dance close very close and I dance on the music and it seems like music is dancing on me and I cover the whole hall, I touch all the floor and I dance and dance till I become one with the music and air and I am held like the petals on the flower and with time, I become fulsome and graceful and live that moment.

And I live my life in that moment. And that's what I call, when I see and live moment to moment, I see my whole life in that moment, fulsome and graceful.

And sometimes, I feel so lazy in that moment, that its possibly the best time for indulgence, indulgence in something I love to smoother or get high on, like just lazing out, or getting my massage done, or just watching the greenery, or just dreaming and visualizing about myself of things that I love, or may be listening to music. Sometimes it could be the feeling of wanting of getting my back touched and warmed up. Or just letting my hair flow.

Or it could be an indulgence in cooking and getting indulged in the same. both cooking and savoring on the food is the best moment for me. cutting that onion and tomatoes and green chilies and the whole process of cooking and frying and sautéing and smelling the food and putting the masalas, the spices and cooking it to right heat and waiting and garnishing it with green coriander is again an indulgence for self and of course savoring it, is amazing experience. Sometime I think that I have become so full and complete in myself by living on my own, that I feel complete and feel no need of anyone else in my life. It may be only when me and my other significant half also feels the same and we give a lot space to each other, and not cross each others lines, do I see the possibility of staying up together.

And then, when I go through this experience in life, times, when I pick up my books and read through and when I find that maybe its getting too erratic, I keep the book aside and switch off completely and start something else to kick me off from my plane.

Times when I felt, is indulgence same as living every moment. Is indulgence same as living completely, Is indulgence same as love with the moment. Is indulgence same as liking what one loves to do. Is indulgence getting aware of all senses, is indulgence same as romance with life. Is indulgence same as getting high in life and then is indulgence short lived, so then, what is life long indulgence with life. Sometimes indulgence could be painful and hurting. Indulgence always may not be numbing the senses.

May be indulgence for a moment could be very very sensory, like taste sense for a while or may be craving for the skin for a while, or may be the visual sensory for moment, may be this is indulgence for a short while, then what is life long indulgence. I feel that once one has to live in the moment, indulgence will also mean, how to get involved life long, cos if one can indulge in a moment one also knows how to extend it to next moment and to next and to next and to next and so on and life long.

However there is a thin line dividing the laziness with indulgence. Laziness is just sensory and sensuous, whereas indulgence means mind also gets involved, when one is lazy, ones mind is passive and when one is indulged, ones mind is very actively involved, in what one is doing.

And this may be same as what is momentary and what is living in a moment. There is a hell lot of difference between the two, although, they may be same. Its like what last for a fraction of second and may not be permanent, is momentary, like the flash of lighting is momentary, like the fear is momentary, but when one jumps in the pool or does bungee jumping is momentary, that fear is momentary, but living in the moment may be that flying only for few minutes, but you live completely in that moment, you do water skiing, you have momentary fear of water, however once in water it vanishes and when you actually water ski for a while you live in that moment.

Like when you see a movie and it's just in that one scene you live the complete moment. Like when I flew over the military camp for the first time in a two seater, I lived completely in that moment.

And as I go along I think to think what it is with me. What I am for long and for short.

And my mind wanders to search and seek, what one does for a moment, is that's someone does on long term too, if so, how important is living in the moment, and then another moment and then another, cos our mind chooses and decided moment to moment, and it always in the choice that we make in that moment of time, that's gives our next moment in life and so I tell myself, go on, live that moment completely and live moment to moment ! Indulge!!

XXVI.   It's not about, someone liking us

Its not about, someone liking us and we liking someone, that's the most simple thing that can happen in life, cos if someone loves and likes you and respects you and you reciprocate the same, its not very difficult to make or strike a conversation, infact most of the time you do not need to say a thing, cos both are on same plane and think the same and when conversation strikes, it's more of building up on each others ideas and thought process, cos it goes hand in hand. Then its like waves playing together, its like wind moving together, embracing together, it's like the twin of thought in mind and fingers typing profusely.

I think it's about communicating with the person, who has a higher degree of liking, loving, respect for you than you would have for that someone. It's about handling such a relationship, cos one does not reciprocate the same way, as the other person does.

It's when we go through this experience do we build up ourselves; it's when we become the person that we really are. cos its very normal to so called love, or like someone to more or less a degree higher than that person, its when we know this exists and how we respond to that person, cos here we know that the person is more vulnerable than you are and that other person feelings are more sensitive than yours, cos you do not have the same feeling to that extent anyways. Its here how beautifully we handle the other person, does it talk about our maturity and how emotionally strong we are. Cos when we have learnt to take care of other person's feelings, give them respect, without hurting them and honor them and yet to be able to maintain our own self is when we have grown from within.

However I truly believe that the person, who speaks out his heart is always at greater risks of exposure and being vulnerable than any other who does not speak his or her heart out. and I also believe that the person, who does this, is far more mature than any other person, cos I believe that each person, knows in her or his heart about what can hurt him and what not, it is, cos, we are human beings and we have senses and we have a special capability to know what's good for us and what's not, and therefore, when we speak our heart out, we in our heart of heart know where are we coming from and what we are doing and possibility that makes us strong.

Its when we know in our heart and read in someone's eyes that the person likes us and however we may not feel the same, it is then, how we respond to this, do we do this, with respect and care and still maintain ourselves, cos it's the other person, who is vulnerable.

It is also when we someone asks for spending our few moments with him/her, how repulsive we may feel towards that person, knowing his or her weakness, but that's exactly the point! How we respond, cos then we know, do we have big heart or is it that we are not capable of handling such situations. Because if we honestly treat, with love, with everyone, things are simpler and easier and less complicated than it appears to be.

Only when one does this, one feels larger in life and one feels humbler too. And there are not other way to feel good about oneself and larger and humbler about oneself, other than when we interact with another human being irrespective of where one comes from.

For one could be cleaning the streets and on the outside it does look like a humble job, but this person could be more respectful than the person who lives in the bungalow and the person who cleans could be larger in life than the person living in the bungalow.

Means, simply, that one is not large by ones status, but one is larger in ones respect for oneself and love for oneself. One only becomes as humble as ones thoughts can be, one only becomes as loving, as one loves oneself, one only becomes as respectful as one respects oneself, one can only become as likable as one likes oneself, one can only grow as big, as one's thinking Is.

It is when, this starts to happen then, we are ready to live our life to the fullest and live every moment, and accept every one as they see us. When we cannot accept ourselves the way we are, it is usually difficult in accepting someone's else's love & respect for us, it is when we have a situation to be able to deal with ourselves, our emotions and a fight within ourselves.

Its all within us, there is nothing outside, we are, what we are, is the manifestation of what we are from inside. Sometime we meet people who are genuine and respectful, it is cos we ourselves are that way. We meet people who are open minded and large hearted and thus it is we who attract such people.

And so therefore, when I look around very carefully, as to who are my friends and who gets attracted to me, most of time, they are the reflection of who I am and sometime, some people may appear weak or not so good and are still around me, they may be on a different time scale but they are on their way to become just as I am becoming in my journey. Cos sometimes when such people surround us, they see the complete themselves in us and they are around us and therefore to be able reciprocate to such human beings is very very sensitive. It's just that they are on a different time scale; they are catching up with us, so I look very carefully and I am very sensitive to such people. And it is only when such times, when the other person talks to us, do we smile, cos we have been there and done that.

XXVII.   I was only 15 when it was talked about for the first time

I was only 15 when it was talked about for the first time; while I was filling up my form for tenth class examination. cos before that it was never talked or required to know. we grew up in the most normal ways and thank God that our parents never talked about such thing at home, we talked about history and how wars were made, how India won independence and what does Pt. Nehru say or dad always asked to write an essay when it was holidays, or when I grew up and knew I could do more, I went to learn guitar classes. Mom taught us and also taught about how it is to have periods, she did not want any surprises for us in life and wanted me to know and be prepared for the same.

It was only in tenth standard that it came as surprise, cos it had to be filled in the form for writing the Secondary Examination of Central Board Secondary Education. Until now, it never was questioned. It was some sort of mixed feeling and I did not know how to respond to this feeling. I was a cycling to school that morning when I had the form in my bag when I was going to school, still I did not know how I felt, and it just felt labeled. I don't know why.

And then, board exams came and I was busy in studying the exams and was happy to write my exams, it was sheer feeling of working hard and achieving something in recognition in life, I knew I would do good and make myself proud of my hard work and I was very happy to come out with flying colors.

Went on to my options in life and took math and again did two years of hard work, burned mid night oil to get through my School of Planning & Architecture in New Delhi. I truly deserved the school and the seat I believed deep down in my heart. I wrote all my exams of engineering, cos I knew that I did not want to do a normal graduation in the city of Moradabad.

I hated the thought of staying back in town and going thru the normal college and deep down inside I felt blessed and it was my opportunity and my fortune that I could still think and hope that I would get through the engineering colleges, on sheer filling up of the form and ticking the form boxes and the right ones.

However when I got the engineering college, I knew and somehow felt in my heart, how and where I came from. Today my thoughts go back to how I used to feel. May be it was too much for a 18year old to think about and go through in life thinking that one come from a category of living which is considered as "Reserved Category". It was too much for an 18 year old, to listen to what normally people said, esp. when it came to my own friends and how people expressed views about it.

I sometimes wondered, would I have done the same thing if I was born in a different family, perhaps not, cos in our up bringing and homes, we never talked about religion or sects or sections of people or castes, I do not know why but we never spoke, and inherently, I did not see anyone as different and never on the basis of what labels they held in terms of religion or castes, it does not matter really, what matters I knew deep down, is how one thinks and what mattered is how one behaved, and in one's actions.

And I just thought I was just born, happen to be born in the family of co called reserved class, which was labeled and I knew when my parents and my grand parents came from, I think we were more of tribe, I think, cos we were a class of people living in the interior of Himalayas and with less economic background and less education was the reason, we were fortunate to be included in the list of scheduled or listed caste.

Sometimes, I wonder, it was again not my parents choice to be born where they were born, I think human being could be born anywhere and it is not your birth which decides your deed and class and creed, but it your life you make and you action which decides who you are and the choices that one takes in life maketh the man what she or he is.

If it was not for the reservation policy that my grandfather would not have been able to become teacher in that government school, my great grandfather had cattle's and no land to live but taught my father to study and I think passed on the inherited spirit to fight out and survive and think big, no matter what.

My grandfather stayed in the village and then moved on to a small town to teach in a school with his elder son and his wife to stay put for better life and better prospects. His elder son and my father inherited the values and the spirit and it was this spirit which made my father the man he is, the mind that he has, it was his spirit and his thinking his dream that made him a Magistrate.

It was a revolution in our family and is still as of now. My father had to be good and he was excellent and operationally, my father filled that form again and qualifies to be a magistrate, those boxes where you fill in your details of birth and where you come from is like a helping hand for families like us and same happened with me. To get through engineering, was possible cos we had provisions, else honesty I would have been doing something else. I do not know if it is good or bad, when yes, I got through and there was another revolution in the family and slowly our family saw the progress from where we were cattle raisers and farming to building sculptors and where my mother's father was a very big landlord in his area.

However as I came along in the corporate world where they were no quotas I proved that I am what I am, on my own mettle and I loved myself. After that it did not matter where I came from, something which society has made such a big issue about, mentally how much one goes through I know, cos I have gone through it, I was fortunate enough to have my friend talked about it, who told me, how does it matter ! it was not them, it was me, who thought about it in another way, thank god for the hype and divisions that these religions and castes and sects create, it effects people and sometimes I can really get on nerves, for no rhyme and reason, one can go through absolute baseless inferiority complex.

It's a different story, cos I understand and I know and I see and I hear and I listen, it does not matter to me now and I also know how will I bring up my children, its not needed for them, to go through all this. Today I see these things are frivolous and smile, may be its good that I am born in a family and I know what it is.

I wonder how small minds could be of people who talk about religion, caste and creed and discriminate human beings, for how does it matter, who has the control of being born where one is born, I also think who has a control of being born in a rich or a poor mans house, the fact that one is born normal is so important. I only learn that ones life is determined how one thinks and not where one is born, but what one makes his or her life to be, is what IS religion and worship all about.

So what do I say about castes and religion. I do not have an opinion nor any say, cos I know I moment I have a say means I am making excuse and living life of circumstances. And living the life of ones dreams is the life of living life of no excuses. It does not matter at all. So where does the question of any reservations and quotas come from. I think we are not delving with the basic question or not focusing on the right thing, which our value systems and our education and talking about a free enterprise and creating equal opportunism and talk about freedom for self. I think to talk about freedom, one has to free oneself from the thoughts which hold us back or engage us from moving forward in life and in our societies and our families. The rest is the manifestation of our thinking. Our life only gets as big as we think and we aspire and there is not quota or reservation of what and how big one can think for oneself and create a legacy. This is my message to my brethren on both sides, where we have tools to our own disadvantage. The tools are limitations, labeling, discrimination and much more.

I believe that there is an institution of freedom and the right tools are the tools of our values that we imbibe ad pass on our next generation to become free of any discrimination or any low self esteem. A human being who has a high self esteem and high self deserve will lead to freedom of thoughts and action and strength in oneself and others, and it starts from self, at home, in our families.

I realized how and what feelings and thoughts I went through, when I was in school filling up that form, I did not want to fill up, why should I. I realized how useless it was to go through that suffocating feeling when friends in my engineering college talked about reservations and how they lashed at so called scheduled castes and tribes. I used to go through hell, for no reason, and just cos you were born in different family and I in a different, you do not get the right to talk or lash out like that, I used to wonder, how insane one could get, why could one not see the obvious. Sometimes I felt how it must have been in olden times, how cruel and unreasonable could a human, an educated one, get. I realized how useless and small minded it was for someone to come back and tell you that I cannot get married to you cos, we are different castes, and it is so funny. And realized much later in life that these were all excuses on a global level for anyone on both sides to justify ones existence and Be it then.

I am glad that I am able to see through and come out of this so called self caused harassment. I was only making myself a victim of what others thought, for it is always my choice to determine how I think and feel about myself and there is no other truth. Today I can laugh about it and I am glad about the fact cos today I see and this is one of the perspective of how people think and where they come from. Cos one is only big or small by one thinking and there is nothing that holds anyone back and it's a free will to think who you are! And that's the essence of life.

And my thought goes back to when I was in my seventh standard, I was cycling to school early morning and we happen to talk about the caste and esp. the scheduled castes and I remember clearly telling my friend, I wonder why we discriminate or think or see low of schedules castes, cos we are all children of God and there is not difference, so should anyone look upon them differently. I remember telling that I do not believe in all this and I have respect for them in the same way I had for anyone else in my life. That was me, without knowing my own label. It makes me happy to remember this, for somewhere in my childhood, I knew that labels are only labels and not basis of ones existence and life.

XXVIII.   I do not know if this is the effect of my reading "The Third Wave"

I do not know if this is the effect of my reading "The Third Wave" by Alvin Toffler but, I am not sure if I will get married not ensuring that I live the life that I desire, that I will leave my kids behind, that I will ever have to work related to fulfill the cover insecurities and work for status and carry any kind of baggage related to work, cos I know, what, me and husband will work or what my guy will work is active income, we will trade our time with money and that is never replaceable and that is not what I am looking for and that will never bother me and I will never fall into the trap this false security blanket ever in life, after being through all that I am being through.

I mean I am amazed that how the most of the people are not able to see this and are only running from morning day to night only to make the ends meet.

I was surprised when one of my new young colleague told me how she wants to be closer to her fiancé place only to spend some more time, and that they have not been able spend any time together, I told her then, get married and stay together, of course I know its not simple, still. And I wondered, are people not able to see that temporary arrangement of just staying close to each other will resolves the issue. I mean in second wave revolution of industrial age, we let our lives to be determined by what our office timing are, who is our boss and how far is our place of work from home and then the same is repeated by our children and then their children and life overall remains the same.

I mean, why not look at the possibility where our toil brings us passive income, which is possible today and is available to common people why not. Why have our marriages determined by the working hours and have the work factor for important in our lives, our whole life revolves around our times of work and the holiday that the company gives or declares. Why not have our own régime and our choice of work and our own holiday plans. Why have any insecurity in the couple about who is earning how much and how does one make the ends meet.

I was amazed when I came to know when a couple friend of mine, was looking for a maid at home, for a three month baby, cos the mommy wants to go to work. I mean such is the state of the effect of second wave on our minds, that we so much evaluate our worth in the office work we do, what about home, what about baby work, what about putting in the values in the family, what about health of the family and of course, what about the choices in life, to do what one wants to do, when one wants to do.

The majority do not even realize how badly are we being effected by the primitive age of working and effecting our generations, what kind of legacy are we passing on to them.

Why cant we have our freedom, complete freedom, freedom from time holding us down, freedom from the money limiting our options and freedom from scarcity thinking, freedom from insecurity, freedom from fear, freedom from inconspicuous health, freedom from our unwillingness to do something which we do not like to, freedom from our own closed mind, emotional freedom.

Where is the freedom gone, was it there in the first place. Yes, I agree in the first place that it is always survival of the fittest and so many other factors, but then who created all this in the first place, we created in the first place and so much that we are the salves of it, does not make sense. We are just being the slaves of our complexity created and we do not even know it.

I mean, why the newly wedded lot should stay at her mother in laws place, cos the home is small. Why should the home be small, why not a big home, huge house and have no challenges in the first place? Why should either spouse ever worry about the time and consider parents as burden in the old age, I mean, my contention is why have old age home, why not have healthy bodies and healthy minds both for our parents and ourselves.

Who determines all this for us, who created all this limiting factors in the first place? Why not have abundance living, abundance health, abundance wealth, abundance time and once we have all this, most and all most all clutter will go away from life and we can have better living and better values, better respect, better relationships, better choices and just better of everything else in life.

I mean why have any economies parameters decide our life, the way we live. And of course, our lives and the economies are now getting stale, the equations are changing, I cannot work my life on old parameters, whose value itself is a big question mark and is in debate and not working or giving me results anymore.

I am glad that I am able to see all this and thus, am decided on my life with no limitations, no scarcity and just have more choices in life than what comes by default, for my life is already not the life by default, but I choose and design my life and I know it's the first step to my freedom. Sure the path is not easy but so is the path not easy, of, by default too. It's always a choice to find a new way of living and have some fun along the way.

XXIX. Setting free

How is it that one stops ones parents to stop desiring things out of their children, they labored. The fact that parents labored for children, does not mean that they own their lives and their future. Also the fact that parents are the parents of children or an individual, does not mean that parents have to be overwhelmed about their off springs responsibility.

There comes time in our lives, when we have to stop feeling or being responsible for any one else's life. By the end of the day, its one life and ones centered self that's the highest religion and that's it. I think if we hold our self responsible for someone's else life means that we still have desires within us, for us, that is not fulfilled and we therefore want the same to be fulfilled by another media and it could be very very true in terms of parents and off springs relationships. This is what constraints the relationship between the parents and the off springs. Perhaps the most responsible thing that an individual could do is to let go off of any relationship, cos that is what would lead to freedom of self and another person.

Its only when in any relationship, we let go off, are we creating, an atmosphere for growth and progress, cos each of us has a soul within and a conscious voice within to guide and to be guided by.

God created every soul with a purpose and when we start interfering with someone's sole and soul purpose is when we start interfering with someone's else's life and that's exactly what causes relationships to go sour, cos no one on earth wants to be told, only for the reason, cos God made a soul with a purpose and our soul does not accept the same when we evolves along with time.

Perhaps, when we see that someone is attempting to influence our soul and our course of life, we at least can become aware of the fact that such and such phenomenon is occurring, cos that's the start of knowing as to what is happening to us and our lives, the first step to detach ourselves from being affected or getting into the phenomenon of getting into someone's else's desire for us and we getting into the wave. This we owe to ourselves and our soul, without getting into the moral science of anything or without getting into any ethical and so called other words which human being invented for their convenience. Simply because, we in the end, hold ourselves responsible for our own actions and consequences.

As a human being, we have a via media to come to this earth through someone's, who bears us, however the bearing does not mean to hold on, from either sides of the bearings. To hold one to ones bearings on either side means not growing up and constraining ones soul. Cos, the soul was free and will after some time become free and the soul is meant to be free, so we do not grow our full selves when we do not let our soul free while on this earth. We owe this to our soul.

As outside we look, with via media or tool like our eyes, our ears and our tongue and our body, our legs and our hands and our actions, only are created to help the core of us, that is our soul to be free, every action we do or take or think, and we could think about this, whether sets our soul free and higher and higher or does it constrains our soul and our energy, and we can feel this, within ourselves, cos our soul is living, breathing and talking to us, all the time and we know this deep inside through the voice of our conscious, who keeps talking to us, and that why its simple, when people say that they go by their conscious voice or some who say that they cannot hear their conscious any more. Well, I would say, that if we look back and if we look now and step outside ourselves and see how do we and how did we nurture our soul.

The moment something inside us is not in sync, we know it immediately and that's the time, we take immediate action or change of thoughts not to let our soul get effected, cos our soul is like our internal engine or torch within which guides us in life, as to what is the way out or where to take the navigation in case we get lost in the process.

The best part is when we are ready or open to listen to our soul, the soul is always very very sensitive to the same and talks and guides and leads and holds. Our soul is like the genie in the bottle, if the bottle is given some air to breathe to be in there, it is at rest, if not, the genie either breaks open or will sleep within. And the same in our souls inside.

And sometimes, the best way to keep our souls alive is to listen to self deeply within. Sometimes, to listen to our souls within, may not be always so simple, that's the time, we start looking for the manifestations outside. Cos sometimes, when deep down, when we know we are looking for something, comes to us in the form of someone saying something to us, or the read in the book that we pickup, or even nature teaching us in her own small ways. So to be aware of our surroundings and others and what we read or talk or others talk, we can immediately know, if that's what's our soul desires, cos the moment, we come across what our soul desires, we feel strong within, as that's the force of the soul looking for and what we seeking from within. It can be called a soul energy or soul chemistry, cos it can be very very scientific and any positive force felt within, therein, is the truth.

And this is when we read the core of any via media of what God made us for, it could be through teachings of Allah, of Bible, or Vedas, or Upanishads, it could be through the emancipation of when one sings, or dances, when one reaches ones higher self, with only self and no one around, cos that is the real connect from within, of within, by within.

Sure, this is not easy, for if it was easy, we would not have emerged as shining gems, it takes work to reach the highest for self and take work to be close to ones soul. It is simple, but not easy, Simple, why, cos, once we just start listening to our voice within, one at time, we walk and act on same, it simple. Similarly, once we are close to what our inner voice has to say, we are protected and know deep within, when we are not listening, so its simple to do this. One step at time. And to look for experiences which leads us closer to ourselves, our soul, and our inner voice. And we develop this, the experiences in life becomes simple, as we are able to look, to hear, to see beyond the obvious and its helps us to be better human beings and in the end, to set our souls free, which we owe to ourselves.

XXX. *Isn't It*

Isn't it amazing how every day gets better than the previous day? Isn't it amazing the life keeps getting better every day? Isn't it amazing that God takes care of HIS creation more than we would ever think of taking care of ourselves.

And may be that's why we must allow God to work on his plan and embrace whatever comes our way and who ever comes our way. If life was a path, through oceans, seas, mountains, deserts and jungle, flowers and snow and land, and when we, ever, reflect on our life, we realize that God made us travel through that path, through the dark nights of the jungle, through the waters of the rivers, through the mountains trails and through the caves and through the desert and the oasis and through the flower valley and through the land of greenery and chirping birds and colorful flowers and bright sunshine.

There were days when it was dark night and there were days when it rained and rained, there were days when moon was full and there was days when the wind blew very strong, there were days when the waves rose high enough, and there were days when rainbow came down from home of God and touched the lives of human being and this earth.

Reflecting on this, I am feel so thankful for every path, for every step that I was lead by and lead into and came out into, cos each step made me and prepared me for the next step, for God had and has a plan for every step that I took and its just falls in place when I look back and therefore each days keeps getting better and better and I am awed by God's plan and I feel blessed and I 'feel loved and I feel secure and I feel deserved by God's Showering of blessings, and how God is preparing me, to be the person that He created me to be.

I also learnt how when I started trusting GOD and trusting myself in the process, everything started falling in place for me. How when I was thankful to God, did, God had his eyes on me. How when we put in our efforts, how HE leads us the way for us, how HE wakes us up, even we missed the alarm in the morning, how HE leads our ways in His small little ways.

For I live a day and in that one day, I am close to Him, makes my day better than every other day. How when I decide and control and then how God rewards me with, in the end of day, with the feeling of, feeling great about myself and have a sense of achievement and accomplishment throughout the day.

I pray and thank God for this and ask for his divine sight and holding and guide me throughout this endeavor. I am also so thankful to God, about how he brought people in my life, who have impacted my life for better, helping me to be the person that I am born to be. for I am sure, there is God within each one of human beings who came and who are in my life, making me the person He created me to be. There were lessons to be learnt from every individual and every aspect of life.

It awes me to get up with a feeling of saying to myself "Yes!!!" to get up and look forward to the day. Taking each day, one at a time. And celebrating each day as it goes by.

XXXI. Basics non-negotiable

Basics cannot be negotiated. Home is home and is the first school, no matter what. My every aspect will be what I am at home. How I respond to at home, and period. My instinct to be at any situation will have its deep root at home, most of the time, it will how I respond and behave at home. As how I can be different with different people, if at home I am what I am. My most comfort zone is at home and even if I am different with different people outside, what I reflect on most of time, how I am at home, cos that will be my answer to most of what I am outside, after some point of time.

No matter how good or bad we are outside the walls of our home, we derive our basics from home. And this process is non stop, from home where we are born to, the home where we give birth and if one sees unstoppable phenomenon, its is a thread which has been running from ages and ages, cos, we are what we are of what gets passed on to us, and most of the time, we choose to be different from what we acquire and only at such times does the history changes it course.

It may be a very slow process and that's how it looks like in the beginning, and when we decide to change courses of our lives, does the history of our family starts changing. Now if this thinking or pattern is common in many families and then in the town and then in the city and in state, does the future of a country changes. Hence if we see any country's future either growing or detoriating, we can tell easily by looking at its people, at their families, cos that is the unit of the country, one can tell whether its values are preserving or de preserving.

That's why some said that my home means a world to me, cos that's where the waves of changes are born, cos each family or in Hindi language "a kutumbh" gives birth of forces, values, uphill of progress. And simply, I understand that my first school, my first business ethic starts from home. A business will only flourish, if I am respectful at home, if I am committed at home and if I take responsibility at home, if I am not taking of doing these things, I will not be able to run business. Or even vice versa, if I am doing all this is my work and my business will I also do the same, I cannot be two people, for if I am two people, at same time, then I am lost and I do not know myself.

For principles of success are same everywhere, whether at home or running a business of being a wife or growing the plant and supporting it. Basics will remain the basics always an that's the law of nature.

It's when I started understanding my mother, did I start valuing myself. It's when I started caring for my father, did I develop respect for men outside home and started having better relationship with them.

It's when I started knowing my brothers strength and weakness, did I start being sensitive to men outside. It's when I knew that my sisters primary love language is act of receiving gifts, did I understand and took her the way she is and understood the finesse behind it.

I do not have to understand the whole world to become wise and humane, I have to only know and understand and respect my own family to know the whole world, and that's my basics and my starting ground and my learning ground in life.

Sometime that's exactly what we miss in life, what we do not get at home; we think we will get outside. For if we could not search the same thing at home, how can we attract the same thing outside our home, for if we are looking outside our home, chances are others too are looking outside, home and may be more and more are looking outside home. so how are we suppose to find what we are looking, cos we left our major learning at home and chances are others too left their learning at home, so by hypothesis, how will we ever find what we are looking for, for most of us left our learning half done at home itself. Home—where we left out on the basics.

May be that's why its called the basics and God gave the perfect environment to learn and to grow, cos at home, we forgive and we love and we learn as we grow, cos home is ground where we do not win against each other, we only want the best for each other, home is the ground for win—win, there is no loose situation here.

Home is the ground God created to be our best and reach our best and may be if we do not have a healthy background of our home, is the gift in itself, cos GOD wanted us to handle tough situations and emerge as better human beings and then spread this outside, taking this light of learning with us to the world outside home.

So may be we are blessed to have a place called home, where no one judges anyone and no one has an option to step out, cos it's where we start and where we end our day, no matter what.

XXXII. It's the thought that counts, from where comes everything

Was standing by the side of the local train holding on to the pillar and my hair flowing in the wind across the train . . . as I walked out of my office that day, I picked up a red flower, lovely and looked at it, it seemed as it smiled at me, whether it was a smile of familiarity cos I was wearing red blouse and red silk long scarf and my trousers. Seemed like it was delighted to see the reflection of the same color that even the flower was wearing.

Standing by the side of train, I was holding my bag, my flower, my cell and my walkman. I was amazed, how much my small hands could hold. I was amazed at the grip of my hands, the curve of the fingers and the small strength with which I was holding everything and yet comfortable with myself and my surroundings. What if at any time, the grip loosens out, or my fingers does not hold the way it is holding up.

I was amazed by the way body construction is made and the way it is all coordinated by the brain, and runs by the heart. One's mind talks thru the skin. How one can feel the warmth of the heart and speaks the mind when we hold someone's hands. Or caress someone, or pat or put a hand on someone's shoulder. how much difference does it make, when a mother holds a child close and physically. It just amazing to see how emotions and feeling talks through skin, through, our touch, through our fingers, our hands, palms, how emotions can get converted, its amazing science. How an intangible can get converted into something so tangible. How ones thoughts can get converted into action and how ones minds speak through the body and face.

How can one see more in someone's eyes and read so much more, how can the line on ones face can tell more about the person, then the speech itself? How can silence speak more than words? How can all this intangibility get converted into tangible energy. May be primarily, everything is just energy, its all an idea, a thought, and then every thing else is just a manifestation of the thought itself, everything that we see around is nothing but a thought converted into physical form, tangible form, does it mean when we see things, or view things, we look at the thought behind it and not so much at the thing itself, cos the thought is more powerful, it's the energy.

And may be also, when we capture a thought, its no more a free energy flow, it gets captured and formed and may be after point of time, this energy needs a release, a new form, as during the span of time and space, the energy captured, or frozen needs a release and a new breathe.

And that's why we believe in so much about the energy around anything in life, any object, any book, any person, any flower, any building, any painting, cos its nothing but the energy captured, or energy converted, cos it all starts from the though which one cannot see, and eventually takes shape of tangibility.

Means, also, when any tangible thing is converted into something intangible, it may loose some energy or possibility that it may also gain some energy. However, one intangible remains only intangible, energy form, it may be pure, and as it is. May be that's why feelings when conveyed as feelings, like silence reciprocated as silence is so very powerful and pure. Vision when reciprocated a vision is so powerful and pure and uninterrupted and untouched.

I think that when one becomes spiritual, because it is very powerful and pure and cleansing and that's why the relationship with Allah is so powerful, because, its one intangible energy meeting another intangible energy, and since this intangible energy is so powerful, we end up feeling exalted, pure and clean ourselves and this feeling is intangible and therefore, the best form of energy.

And when any energy takes shape of tangibility, it may loose its original form. Therefore, one needs to be very very detailed about ones thought and its little component getting transformed and may be therefore we say that weak thoughts will results into something which will not last long and is very fragile. And it only strong thoughts which would mean strong energy and which would result in the closest connection with the strong thought will result into strong shape.

And may be that's why when a body stops functioning, there is a release of the energy, its only the body which is gone and which had to go, cos like I said with the span of time and space, the energy conserved, or frozen, or converted needs to get a release, and when its high time, the energy decides or just that the energy gets released automatically, and we say that the person is dead, why don't we say that the energy in the body got relapsed, cos that's what is happened, in this case.

And may be again a energy gives rise to so much of other energies around us, as in coordinate of space and time, energies are interacting with each other and producing another form of energy and therefore, if we see the universe as a continuum of energy, it may be explosions of energies in the universe and that's how the creation of different objects keeps happening and may be all this energy is emanating from some main source, that light, that Main energy is but Allah.

True, it's all about the interplay of energy and may be that's why we must really learn to listen to energy and energy within whose name we also have given a conscious. Cos that is the fountainhead of pure energy within, from which everything, every thought comes and from where all conversions outside, in tangible and intangible form is effected and goes into.

Hence to choose any energy around us, within us, is where our sense of energy comes into play, so as to protect the purity of energy within us. To continue the pure thought, to continue the aligning of the Main Energy with our energy and hence, be light and pure, while we go through the manifestation of energies within and around on the larger scale of Creation. And all this comes from a thought, the source, As thought itself is the strongest, the most powerful energy within.

XXXIII. *Angels*

And yet I am amazed when it was only written on the books, as I had never personally experienced this. I experienced this very strongly in last couple of days, the fact that thoughts change everything for a human being. It's the thoughts that count in making up the person and also deciding how the person is mentally, physically, emotionally.

I was not well and had developed a very high fever and had to rush back from the office. I realized it so strong that I had to get well as I had few important assignments coming up in the next couple of days ad I had to get back in shape, come what may. When I came back home, I slept off like a log and ate like a hog when the dinner was ready. After the iftaar in the evening, I drank water like a camel, storing some water and ate like a hungry child sitting in my kitchen.

I slept off early and attended the only call of my friend in the night. When I slept off. I got up in the morning and had already decided to give myself rest that day. After the Sahiri, and the Fajr ki namaz, I read Hadis and then went off to sleep, only to get up late morning. I read a lot that day and it was Allah's gift to me that day, I personally received the Reading Book from N21 and I started to read this new fresh book, I was longing to hold in my hands. That book was magic, it just gave me new energy, new smell of pages and something new for my mind to remunerate on. I think these small things are but planned by Allah.

I went to meet one of the old friend who had shifted back to Mumbai and then, went to take a walk in the gardens and swing in the swing for a long one hour I suppose, it was a bliss to swing in that swing that late eve and I felt like a child, with smile and happiness back on my face. I met my friend on my way back home and had dinner and felt at peace.

After Isha ki namaz, I retired to bed, called my friend and spoke little on phone and then decided to sleep off. I was at so peace that day. There was thoughtlessness and I was so blessed to be in that state. I thought to myself, just as fast is to cleanse the body, so is thoughtlessness to cleanse the mind.

How worked we become sometimes by just thinking so much, planning so much and sometime mind gets into chaos and so much thinking, that one only wishes, if there was, a switch button to thinking and non thinking mode, one could have used such a device.

And that night I had no sleep in my eyes and I loved the silence of the night. I experienced how sometimes blankness of thoughts could be a bliss and emptiness of mind, means no chaos in mind could be so eternal. Silence was serene that night, until I slipped into the arms of sleep. I talked to the angels that night, asking them to come and near close to my bed and heal me up and kiss me love and see me while I sleep. I thought to myself, that tom morning, I am waking up fine and healthy and happy and will go to work and enjoy my day and enrich my work and day. And that's exactly what happened. And I was but only awed by the Supreme Presence.

My day went off well and I was prepared for the day next day. Things are mostly planned by God and when we say things that happen have a reason, is so very true. My friend had just gone thru a counseling and I was about to go thru one tom, and when I called my friend, it seemed that we both had to experience this together, although there was no connection, however she had to go thru this in her professional life and me in my personal life.

While sleeping I did a self talk telling myself that I look forward to tom, very experience and that My Allah will take me thru, I asked the angels to come and sit near me during the session and protect me. Next day morning I smiled to myself in the mirror and told myself, I am thru with all this, in life, today and today is the new beginning for me, I believed that day was the night of AL QADR and in my heart it said, today I am blessed by this night and its my new life from today onwards. Back in the courtroom during the morning and noon, thing went smooth and seamless and I was back in office, only to meet friend to hug her and get a hug from her, she had little tears come in her eyes when we met and I was just in state of trance I think.

I loved that moment; we had come a long way. Sure, Allah guides us through everything in life and has a purpose in our lives. Only for people to tell in my office that I looked happy and dreamy, I did, I wanted to walk on the ocean that day and talk to the moon and stars and hear the rain drops fall.

Was blessed that day to go over to my couple's friends place to open my roza for iftaar and to be dropped back to station for home. While in my Isha that day, I was overwhelmed and awed by the Creator-Allah and I had tears in my eyes while I offered my Namaz. It was also the night of Al Qadr and I felt blessed.

Next day was diwali and I rested at home like the camel who had walked days long in the caravan in the desert or the bird who had flown for miles together to come back to her nest. The day was symbolic new me. The process had started long back, the closure was finally done. Alhamdulillah!

I also noticed myself remembering the Al-Fatiah during my Namaz, for the first time, I recited Al-Fatiah in my prayers.

XXXIV. *Freedom of my Completeness*

Sitting here on my bed right now is an exalting experience as the mountain cool breeze touches my skin and my bone and the moon peeps from the clouds and the trees sway in the breeze and I can smell the wet earth, it's just an amazing experience.

I am experiencing total freedom right now, freedom on my being, my space, my mind and my soul, I feel free and I am flowing in the experience. I right now, have the choice to remember the same feeling, the good feeling, the great times, my experiential asset I can feel and remember at this point of time, with no attachment.

It's the same wind which touched me when I was in tenth standard and there used to be a wind all of sudden with appearance of clouds and the weather would become cool all of a sudden, soaring my spirits and the rain would touch my face in my veranda and I would not know or would explode with my emotions of feeling exalted.

It's the same wind which blew in my college amongst the jungle it was, with river flowing, in the eve, and I would be in hostel, a lot excited and somewhat afraid, as it would get dark clouds and breeze make the sound and the coolness of the breeze would not just get into my skin, but my heart, my mind and my soul. And I would experience complete high and just be it, feeling and breathing in each moment standing in the gallery open in my hostel lobby.

And the same wind would after few years, that I felt, when I was in post graduate hostel amongst another jungle, where we would see the rain drop and sip tea, soaking in every moment.

It's the same wind, I felt across the continent, when in evening it would get cloudy and I would wait eagerly at home, it would be such a fresh breeze, that even my skin would not have ever known before, the sky would be deep dark blue with clouds holding them, the wind would swoosh away my fantasies and I would sit at the verandah outside in the cane chair, holding me up, holding up the moment inside me, the wind in my body, the exalted feeling I would get, with winds taking me higher and higher.

Today, as I walked past the flower market in matunga, I was drowned by the fragrance of the flowers and I looked up to see the sky, at the dark grey clouds on the back ground of huge old trees and lamp posts with some deep yellow color and I thought to my myself, wow, this is amazing, this is the moment, and this is the time.

I felt free, like the feather flying in the air, I felt literally felt light, like the air rising up with the breeze, my heart opened up more and more to take as much as I could, to soak in as much as I can and I smiled at everyone passing up, perhaps they thought I am in love.

I was in love with the moment, with the breeze, with the chill that was brushing against my skin, getting into my body and bone and in hair and in my eyes and in me completely. What more, I smelled the wet earth as I walked past by, to take the train to home, to lift myself from the ground, seven floors above and as I sit here, with cotton sheet on my legs, I feel the cold, I feel the chill, I feel light, I feel light, I feel happy, that I am able to completely rejoice this moment, for myself and do not look forward or hold on any other being, for my happiness, its me and my moment, and that's freedom and freedom of my thoughts, freedom of my completeness, of what I choose to remember and cherish and feel great about.

XXXV.   Repeated Experiences

When certain experiences repeat, there is something to learn from them, for if we do not they keep coming back. So when this was happening to me, I started to think, why this is again and again occurring to me, I am sure apart from other physical manifestations, I have something to learn from here. And it all happened with my eye becoming sour again and again and I realized, that I need to listen to the need of my body, of how it feels strongly it needs to be treated and what it is responding to and what's it is retaliating to.

The one thing I picked from Paolu Coelho book, is not always self remedy is a good thing, there is a science of medicines too and it may to some and sometimes to large extent help. What I learnt is that sometime, with all the combinations, of thoughts and physical exercise and some touch of medicines and also the food that we eat, all combination that is acceptable to our body, can lead to a overall healing and not just one method or one of way of healing, cos it is then the body responds in the most responsive manner, cos may be the thoughts are required to remain calm, may be reading of some books are needed to divert attention and keep fruitfully engaged and also at the same time, getting some ideas, for if we are looking for something it sure does comes in the manner of book, or someone saying something, or any newspaper lying on ground and speaking something to you, and may be also in form of prayers, cos prayers gives us hope, hope to keep faith and patience and we having our deepest conversation with God, cos He is the best to have any conversation with, or may be also the kind of food that we eat, it does reflect in our body and our system and has an impact, and then the medicines will work best in such an environment, as then, our body, mind and our thoughts are most responsive and we create an environment where medicines just cures it and does its work, besides other work being done for us.

And this is exactly, somewhere I has lost patience and was slipping into a sympathy state for myself, its then I decided that let me give myself my time, cos its shouting for time from me, its crying for attention and I must not ignore and gives all my time, my quality time to it, cos it is one of the admired part of my body and my face. So I decided to give it some time I took care of it, by washing it with hot-warm water. I applied slaiva to, as it a natural cure for any wound, and then I relishes the greenery in front of me, it was like the treat to my eyes, and then, I washed my face and applied some cucumber paste to it, for cooling and also put some eye drops. Before this I had read enough and I just came across exactly what I was looking for. it touched my soul, somewhere, I also realized that I came across what exactly what I thought and believed in, sometime, we need just a re-iteration in life, some reflections and that's exactly what I got, in the book of Paulo Coelho, the book name—like the flowing river.

I only bought the original of this book, only in the honor of the book (a thought ran in my mind—when I write a book, I would love people to read the original print, although reaching people is more important, still, the original is the one, so why should I pick my favorite authors book in paper back and discounted of photocopy version, do unto other, as you want them to do to you.

So, I read and read and then read the Kitab and it gave me direction and strength, as it always does, every time and then,

I spend sometime with the lady who comes to pick up my clothes for ironing and she spoke about her grandson and her daughter (daughter in law) and I could make out the genuinity through her talks.

Here was a perfect example of someone who had pure heart and how one's adversity combines them as a family, and this was possible only cos there was love in the family and the two women were full of love and their combined their goal in life to make it together in this world. I learn so much form this family. it was most mother in law and daughter in law relationship I had seen, so much of love and bonding, even after when the mother's son had passed away due to heart attack and who was the loved husband of the daughter in law.

She taught me how despite day to day challenges work has to go on and how they cared for each other. This is called empathy, what we read, learn and are trained in the corporate, we can learn from people around us. and that's exactly what she gave me, we shared a little joke amongst us and then she carried on, I could not help but to stand at my door, admiring this lady, until she was lost into the staircase leading down and into the lift of the building. With all these experiences, I said to myself, hey I must also touch my eye with love and not with anger cos I care for her and that I am so grateful to her for being the most lovely eyes to me, helping me to see the world and seeing the unseen, on this earth.

Slowly and steadily I felt that I was feeling better in my eye and it was getting healed and it only needed some attention in life and some love and care from me. And that it had been fighting for the attention. Also, I learned to listen to how my body was responding and what it needs at the most, now.

Right now, sitting here on my window, when I told my senior that I am going to see my doctor, what I meant was, this Dr., this caring for self and that my books and my greenery down in my only doctor and that the eye drops is my doctor and my friend. Sitting here on my window, with the greenery down and sun basking on them, I feel nice, as I am able to absorb the time and the wind that comes and touches my face once in a while.

And now its time to pack up and go thru the day, as something's are to be done and cannot wait just because of some speed breakers in life, I have to go over them any way and keep on driving and that's life. And I love life, I admire life and I am thankful to it for teaching so many things, and coming back to teach again, if I didn't learn it the first time. My hats off to the Creator and HIS perfect system.

The instinct of Appeal

I, in the middle of the night just get up and wear my blue wrap around my waist, leaving it a little loose to give a very appealing look and then I just take my blue chiffon Stoll to tie it around my chest to just camouflage it around the cleavage and then tie the knot around my neck.

Then I stand like a model in front of the mirror and sometime I do walk like one, watching myself in the glass of my window and in my mirror. I do then all kinds of dances, which are appealing and like a woman holding the pole and twisting around.

When I have the camera with me, I click me in the most appealing manner and then, get a kick out of watching me on the camera. it gives me a kick, about my flawless skin, about my counters, about the way I look when I am in blue wrapped around, about how I look when my blue danglers dangle from my ears and how I just tie around my hair at the back, carelessly with some flicks just left around to be blown away with the breeze and the wind of the fan that blows . . . it just feels nice, this may not be necessarily linked with the feeling of making love or having sex, but the feeling of seeing oneself in lesser clothes and yet look so appealing, looks like a fantasy taking shape. It feels nice to be watched over by men and women admiringly, by people, who love and appreciate the good things in life.

It's a deep desire of any women to look appealing, in some or the other age of hers. It starts right from a age of five or a four year old, when you start seeing a very little girl dressing up or putting or applying makeup, it could be imitation of mothers or sisters or significant others and this continues through our her life A little girl, a school girl, growing girl, a teenage girl, a college girl, a young woman, a dating girl, a working girl, a married girl, a mid age woman and a old girl, notice closely, she has this deep desire to look beautiful, she has this deep desire to look appealing, and crudely somewhere, she has a deep desire to skin it down.

She somewhere carries this fantasy as she grows up, sees TV or watch movies or see love being made or even sees woman walking on the ramp, or sometime may even see women on the beach, or may even just see woman any age who has a beautiful skin, has a lovely hair, has slurry eyes, has a radiant skin and has a shapely body, the woman, when she sees this will have only two feelings, she will not have a neutral feeling s, either she will despise this or she will fantasize herself there.

Either feelings, are feeling of wanting to be appealing. This may nowhere be connected to sex or getting on to the bed or even getting physical, but this may be deeply connected to looking just appealing, getting the glances, getting noticed, getting admired about the way she is, it is from men and women, that's what it is.

I think its just that most of us women do not dare to look good or just pretend that we do not care enough and that looks really do not matter, as a matter of fact, sometime we may have given up on looking good so early in life, that we no longer kindle to our feelings of tenderness and looking good and appealing, cos I am 100 % sure, every woman at some point of time in life does think and tries to be looking good.

Now this may not or should not be related to any ill feelings or judging any woman on this ground, and in fact I would lash out to those women and men, who will start to bring in the perspective of moral or ethics here, or even respect denominator here, for the factor of appeal has nothing to do with either of these, for the men and women who are doing this great blunder, are those men and women who are either control freaks or who themselves, have sex on their mind, straight off or who are craving for this freedom, they are men and women, whose either childhood has been very very moralistic and judgmental, they possibly have still not accepted their sexuality and their bodies and may be somewhere they despise the way they look or are either badly "wanting" to break out of their shell, and hence, when they see someone like this, their defeat or unhealthy self starts to talk o them and it is usually difficult for them to accept the truth that its okay and great to look good.

The truth, is a man and a woman are created on a very basic level to be appealing to each other, and that the animal instinct and if men and women are not living this instinct, they are lying to themselves. Because this is the first thing that attracts a man or a woman. Think of how many good friend of opposite sex, you and me had and what's the first thing that appealed to us, most of us honestly would admit that it's the vibes or the physical attraction that pulled each other to each other.

And believe me that feeling is very good and infact it feels great. That's the first step to curiosity towards each other, between a man and a woman, ask any good friend of opposite sex after years of knowing them and find the answerers by yourselves. My self have such good friends, buddies and I know that either its their eyes, or the way they looked, or an appeal in them or their strong vibes which has attracted me to them and it only after this initial attraction I have become good friends with them.

And today they are my great friends and I still do care how I look when I am with or for that case wherever I am, I care how I look and feel. Even when I am sleeping, as when I sleep I desire to feel lovely and beautiful, sometime, I wear by cleanest clothes which feels nice on the skin and put perfume and sleep, as if it's the date with sleep, after all, I have this date and this closeness for the rest of night, I better feel good about myself.

Another fact, a woman when she is with a man and makes loves, and this stands for both a man and a woman, in the most intimate moments wants to, desires to, look appealing, in the most initial stage of love making, does, a man and a woman want to look appealing to each other and this feeling in mutual, to start to make love, or even in the playfulness of making love with each other.

And this is a fact that every woman in her life makes love to a man and so does a man (barring few, although, I would say, its deep desire of every man and a woman, it all started from there, the Adam and the Eve) and its this moment that makes us fantasize and desire and drives us to look lovely and appealing and beautiful, and this is a natural law, see the animals and you will find the truth, how they attract each other and call on each other, how the heat builds up, how they go high on calling on each other to make love. And we are human being with some brains; we would but want and love to look appealing for this reason, possibly the strongest reason.

Some of us take this feeling of looking appealing, in public, whereas some of us limit to our living rooms, some carry it everywhere and I think its just fine with what we do with ourselves to look appealing, some even keep this, very private only to themselves and feel happy about the fact that they look beautiful and I think we can just leave it at that, how we construe about what one is doing with it and how the rest of other take out meanings and manifestations out of this would be getting into moral science class and judgmental mode here and spoil the whole fun of just looking appealing.

Honestly it does feels nice to look appealing, I would say it enhances the self esteem of a person and the confidence of a person, after all, would you not like it if people give you admiring glances when you walk down the street on a day of your work to office, you would, wouldn't you, so why hide the fact, go ahead and look appealing, it would the tough day for them, who will not be able to take it just the way it is and extend their manipulated minds, anyway, who cares. the for there is always a paretos law applicable everywhere, some will really admire you and get attracted to you and some will want to dress you down anyways . . . no matter what !! So be it.

The woman wears the burkha or duppatta or veil not because she loves to wear it, but because she is just not comfortable with some glances or has some fear of those glances, given the fact that this fear is not there she would love to let her hair flow, and their radiant skin show and wear the most elegant attire and even if the skin shows, it would not matter, cos deep down, she would know and she knows, she is being admired or she looks appealing when she walks that way . . . .

Like I would love to wear a shapely saari to work. I would love to wear the blues when I am on the beach, I would love to wear my sleeveless and wrap around in the summer, I would love to wear the most lovely swimming costume when I get down in the pool, I would most of all love to look appealing, for sex is not my mind, for I know when I am with my guy what matters most.

I am going ahead and look my most appealing to myself, for once I love, myself and that way I look, rest is only a mirror!! I would only say indulgence in self is sometimes healthy, very healthy!!

XXXVI. Evolution

And as I write from four lines to ten to more and more

And as I read from a thin book to mid size book to larger

I evolve too, for I think that there is always a baby step to everything that we do in life,

We learn to recognize the alphabets first and then read and write the alphabets and then go to words and sentences, so how in life can we ever expect ourselves to jump on to what we are made and brought out to this world, every day is an evolution, and with time we evolve anyways, we do not have a choice, now the only thing that is in our hands is that we being aware that we are evolving as a human being every day and we become participative in this process and somewhere begin to enjoy it and like ad love it and may be sometime we become observer and sometime we just flow with the flow of evolution process and hence the key of energy is to go with the flow and not against the flow, and when we start doing that, we start finding ourselves full of energy and forward energy or else when we go against the process of evolution is when we experience the negative energy and the body is like a litmus paper, it will immediately throw signal at us, when we are going with the flow or against the flow of evolution of everyday process.

And sometimes, when we are open and most of the times when we are open and just follow our instincts, are, when nature starts working for us and with us.

It just directs us to the right taxi wala and the right person at the ticket counter of the station and to the right way of approaching the bookshop and to the exact book falling in our hands, that's how nature works and that's how the instinct works for us and with us.

Whenevever in doubt and contemplation, I sit near the ocean, so that I can have my freedom of expression and let loose myself, become small very small in front of the large expanse of water, is when I start to become one with nature and start listening to what the nature has to tell me and I just follow it, and it becomes my guide. that's why most of the times when I am with nature, whether its an ocean, or travel far off places to mountains or even just look out of my window to see the rising sun, I listen, I watch and feel inside how I feel and just take off for the day, and it guides me in disguise and it rests inside me a an energy bag and my compass to guide me thru the my day, thru people that I deal with and come in touch with. That's why I keep going back to nature, cos deep down, I know when I become the disciple of nature, I am in safe hands and my journey becomes joyous and free, I can be what I am meant to be. I am on the right path. And so I take out time to be with the nature, with the things that makes me light and free.

For the I also realized the worst plight of any human mind is when one thinks of something in their mind and does not do the same, for our minds knows what it wants and wishes and aspires to, however, we do not wear the same as our mind on us, is when we start to live a painful lives and thus effect the environment around.

Now this can be overcome, when we realize that nature and us have something in common, we have a free spirit and we are made of same elements, when we start to spend more time with nature, the more of our core elements begins to blossom and thus our mind, body and soul begins to recognize the elements in us and that's when the nature starts to work for us and gives us the raising board to jump up or dive into the swimming pool of our lives and journey.

And as its simple to watch the nature, the greenery, the raindrops falling, the sun rising, the ocean waves rising, the birds flying and chirping and the moon shinning, and it's the most easy and simple to be one with nature, that's why such simple steps, baby steps makes it simple to anyone who understands this and realizes that how simple it is follow ones self and discover oneself, as, it just takes one baby step to start enjoying the nature till the time, we start realizing it within ourselves and then once we have done that, to go with the flow of nature and ourselves too, and this unlimited relation keeps us going for the best of us, making the nature one with us and someone whom we can always rely on when we are in midst unknown.

And this is evolution of self, this is evolution of nature within ourselves, and only when we allow, this nature and natural evolution, do we blossom in our lives and other too.

XXXVII.   Isha Ki Namaz

Life as it is. Life is full of possibilities and warmth. Life is worthwhile and is progressive. I believe that there are no coincidences in life. Allah speaks to us, in the language of nature, which we call omens; it is up to us, to pick it up and follow the path of Allah, thru the language that He is talking to us. Like we were just talking about AynCis, which is the Ain of Surah 19, Mariyum.

And when I was performing Isha tonight, I opened the Quran in the last rakaat, and it was Surah 19 which got opened and I read what is Ain. This is not a coincidence it is the light of Allah, it is the blessing of Allah. He speaks to us in HIS language, Sometime, when we are aware of ourselves, we recognize this sounds and sights and when we are not aware of ourselves, we are not able to pick up the signs of Allah.

And the language which keeps us close and aware of ourselves is the language of Love. Love for ourselves and love for future, only then we are able to understand the universal language, the language of Allah, The One and The Only One! And what takes to Love ourselves, in the first place, is to, accept ourselves, the way we are, the Way our parents gave birth to us, the way Allah created us. It is only when we accept ourselves, the way we are, do we love ourselves, do we respect ourselves, do we allow the child in us, to play around and be young and are so much ourselves. Do we then, listen to what our heart has to say to us.

For, it takes the angel to protect us, when we are as innocent as a child, do we allow the angels to protect us and allows us to converse with them. For sometime, the language of nature, may be the language of the Guarded Angel who protects us in the all the times.

Therefore, in the humdrum of life, we need some time in complete solace with ourselves, to listen to ourselves, to allow ourselves to be lead by the Angels and become one with our soul, which Allah gifted us, when we came to this earth and it is through this language of soul that ALLAH speaks to us.

Sometimes, the best way to brings ourselves back to our heart is to read the life of Prophet (Sallallahu Walaiva Salaam) and it brings us to the space in which our heart is purified through the readings of Prophet's (Sallallahu Walaiva Salaam) and His Life, our life is aligned to the right path.

However, this is a process and it may take sometime, to be really be in peace with oneself. As the journey is inwards and just like when we drive and we keep speeding ahead of unwanted vehicles infront of us and we keep leaving them behind, similarly this journey is an internal one and we may have to keep, speeding ahead of the clutter in our lives and our mind to speed ahead and be on the clear road, inwards, a journey, where our soul starts to understand the language of God, where our mind starts to understand the signs of Nature and therefore Universe and that of Allah.

And sitting here today, I am in awe and little fearful, as when Allah, speaks to you, amongst, zillions and zillions of existence on this earth, Allah, talks to His Creation, He knows of every

Soul He Created and this trembles me with fear and tears that Allah talked through my Soul. He knows, I am protected Child and He sees it through!

Allahmdulillah

XXXVIII.   The music of our Souls

Love and Longings of the lives that we live, and when we know after living very very deep, that life is a pastime here on earth and the life after this life on earth is the real life.

Life here on earth is like the keys of the piano when we experience for the first time, it does not emanate sound that is music, and it may and will even sound irritating for a long time, until we practice it again, for to practice it again and again, we need the music in our minds and in our eyes, till our skin breathes of it and after playing it again and again and making that combinations of what brings in the right cord and right symphony to connect to that music in our minds, is what is called living on this earth.

It aint all beautiful in the beginning, it is infact, very testing and very taxing and very de-motivating, till we learn the music of our lives, while we live on this earth. There would be another souls around, who may mock us at our try, or may be the sounds on the piano keys we are trying to perfect, for they may not see and know and look beyond what they hear, they may ridicule and or even may leave one alone in this struggle of getting the right cord or the music and the symbols. Only those souls and few of them, who have done the art of finding and discovering this music of their lives and have tried it before just like you do, will stand by you and still hear that music, which they can make out, cos it was their piece of music they wanted to perfect at a point of time in their lives.

So go on and practice their music and keep hitting the keyboards and the music will come . . . for only when we play again and again on the piano, we know that importance of each key and what music it plays and what is high and low of each key and then we know and combine the keys and the sequence of making a sound that connects to each, will, the music appear in our mind and outside too . . . the only thing which will keep the music coming, will need for us to listen to our hearts and minds and keep very very close to it, for any distraction may lead us away from the music of our lives and we may take longer to reach the music of our lives and therefore may not receive the labour of our love from attaining the right music of their lives.

And each one of us may and will have different music's of our lives, it is for us to live ourselves a full chance to create our own music of our lives and to be able to become one with it, for each piece of that music will have something to say about ourselves, it will have the undertones of our struggle and the high of the feeling of getting that exalted feeling when we get it right and that's when we start to talk the language of nature and of the universe and does the sun and moon also seem to be dancing and swaying with that music, it's the music of our soul.

And to reach this music is a journey more worthwhile than anything while living on this earth and anything attaining on this earth, for it is this music, which, will make our journey, on this earth simpler and make things and events worthwhile and rewarding, like I learnt that life on this earth is just but a pastime and it is life after this earth, which is a real life, may be, we can then, find our music, while on this earth and when we are no more, it is this music of our soul, which will be either, be complete and will remain with us, or may be this music, will not be complete, will be undiscovered and unsung and we will never ever know, what was the music and the song of our soul when we leave this earth. For when we have found the music of our lives and our soul, we would be able to relate to those, who have found the same for themselves and it would be a seamless orchestra when we are together.

For those who have not found this, will still remain, in the lost group of souls and there will be no music, and may have to come back to earth to again their find music, cos when after life, it's the soul which will remain and the soul without the song will be the lost one and may want to come back, to find its music while on the earth.

The experience in our lives that we go through while on this earth, are the accords and cords of our music, which all falls in place, when we have learnt to deal with them and overcome, for we will know. After such experience, what syllable we get and what cord music we get and the more we experience this, the more rich we become in our library of cords and syllable of music, until in the end, we can play and compose our own music, the music of our soul.

Sometimes, it will take longer to get that right accord of the keys we press in our piano of our lives, for we may not be able to figure out once how much pressure on that key causes what music. It may take us to connect with previous cords and then linking it all together. That's called reflecting in our live experiences and relating it within ourselves, as to see what we need to release from ourselves within, so that we get the right music that we are looking for. for sometime, getting the right cord may take us from within to release something we have been holding back in our lives and therefore not getting the right button ever, or the right pressure in the piano of our lives, once we have released from within, we will get the effect of same in the music of our lives, to be able to connect to the next cord and to be able to generate the link that leads us from our previous cord to the next one, making it seamless, helping ourselves to flow and not get stuck again and again at the same cord, and that's how the journey begins, it begins with releasing from within what we do not want in ourselves first and then around us.

This journey of music of our soul will take long time, will test our patience and we get also get stuck at the same cord again and again, it may bring frustration and may also lead to quitting from finding our music of lives our souls, the only thing that will keep us going is to keep close to our heart and mind to be able to listen to our own music, which no one knows and keep at it, with trust in ourselves and faith in Allah, to help us reach the music of our souls, and when in the end we have attained, there is pleasure in playing the same, for this music, would be yours and only yours, and no body's else's, and the connect to this music, would be is elating and exalting, for our heart will know and our soul would be able to participate in the orchestra of music, of life, we meet after our lives on this earth!!

XXXIX. Difficult for the keeps

And to keep is difficult, its not easy, for when a man marries a woman, the main thing that he is enabling for the woman is to think wild, with a choice at any point if time, the floodgates that he or she is opening for herself and himself, is the gate to ecstasy, legally and ethically, the right to have the freedom of intimacy and closeness like never before, and actually imagine, the limitless intimacy without having to think about any consequences, about any after effects, for even the after effects are a welcome.

And then how come it is not incumbent upon him not to keep this keep(woman of his), for understanding now transforms to knowing, and once the knowing has come to being, can it be denied that time is not needed, can it be not understood that those moments are needed, not only needed, but at times could be demanded and then how can one not keep it, going . . . for, understand that floodgates have been opened and mind has been set to think wild without any boundaries, for there are not suppose to be any boundaries and that's when the most basics form of any male or female comes into being. Is it not then even more crucial to keep this going then . . . to be there together, for each other.

For if at this juncture, if the woman is left alone or for that case even the man is left alone . . . there are all good chances of spill—over . . . it human, animal nature which is at work and the animal being the animal may or could go to any form, for if the imagination has to be satiated, the intimacy is needed, no matter what!!

Then, do not blame either the woman or the man, for if there are any spill-overs . . . happening, for it is only for either and if either one is not there, its not healthy and not to be . . . for there will be other ways to keep it going . . . and that's why I think and believe that how urgent is it, the need of time creation to be with each other, else, what's the point.

It's no point, in blaming later, on . . .

Where were you, when the time was there to be!!

For I believe that once this is taken care, rest all becomes not so difficult, this being taken care of, takes care of many many other peripheral aroma in the so called life, its simple and no rocket science!

XL.   Sometimes giving it any name means justifying it

Relations uncalled for, still existing for the namesake, to give it a name. I wonder, if relationships sometimes and most of times need to be given a name, for I know that the only relation which occurs is your mother and father and brother and sister and rest all is but a maze of confusion and respect and just a coordinate with respect to the (0, 0) coordinate of what one is born to be, or born of, or born by and full stop.

For I still remember that I had liked a guy back in my engineering college, I had actually come to become very fond of him, with nothing in particular in mind, just good little cute friends and it was always a pleasure seeing him walk into the class and sit beside him when the lectures happened and have chai with him.

There was something more than a girl liking the boy, it was that of becoming fond of person and liking his company and just adoring him and that's where it was and it was to be. I always felt protected when he was around and by and by we became very good friends. there was some connect somewhere, until one day he confided in me about how he was crazy about this one girl in the batch and how much he liked her and how could or would he approached her. I was more than happy, cos I could almost see, how it hurt him to love her and how it could have been kept growing in exponentially, each day when he saw her . . . and we set out to fix both of them together and today . . . after so many years . . .

I still remember how they two were so fond of each other, that one day when we were returning from town to our college campus and they stood under the umbrella, talking, only people outside the umbrella knew, that it was not raining and that these two had to be in love not to notice that all . . . and we laughed out loud until they too realized and blushed, those days, the lovers used to blushed . . . and today, they are married and have a small little child.

Rabo and My relation always grew and became stronger and stronger as time passed by, my respect and love for him has only grown and I have only become more fond of him and his wifey and child and that's all . . . in this case, it was perhaps, he felt always in me as his sister whom he missed a lot, and therefore, is my so called brother, however, I feel that we as human beings do not need to define, this relation, for this relation is purely of hearts and love and respect and it only grows. Is it meant to be named, I dot not know, for this is pure and its wonderful to have someone like him in my life . . .

My brothers best friend is someone I always had a lot of talk when I was around and he was around and we had good fun, in fact I liked him and I used to often think of having a Momin for a husband, for somewhere I saw goodness and respect and intellect and gravity of thoughts.

However, I was only an observer, and it was always a fleeting thought, cos I never took it so seriously, however, somewhere in the back of my mind, he had made some impact and we, my brother and me and his friend became very conversant with each other and we just shared and talked and talked till we developed good faith and understanding amongst each other . . . only for me to go away in pursuit of studies and then far away city of Mumbai away from home in cozy and lazy city of lucknow and here I was, time went by, I saw many men in between and explored, I was on total wild, untamed exploring the world and the men and the relationship and the experimentation of anatomy always kept me involved more than I could even imagine.

It was then, after years that I saw and realized that I had tied a knot only to untie again and in the meanwhile, my brother best friend too tied a knot and then we were in touch on email and then he had a child, a sweet one.

And one day I get and receive an email, from my brother best—"hello sister!!!" and I fell off my chair, for it was not for anything else, however, I just found it very awkward and uncalled for, it was something not natural, I was a human being, I had a name and so was he and there was not a need to define any relation in between, it was uncalled for . . . no, it was not that important for me, to even worry or think about this.

And today we are very good friend and his wifey too and his baby too. its just that when I reflect today, sometime, I feel that there is no need sometimes, to define any relation, cos it would mean that we are justifying the coordinated position, I do not deem it, to be necessary, simply for the fact that, when any relation is pure and out of respect, other than husband and wife, it need not become brother and sister, it could—" Just Be."

For I have a brother and he means the world to me, and I do not think I can replace any feelings towards him, for anyone else. Everyone else, is each of them, just the way they are and my brother is what he is to me.

XLI.   Loveless Relationship, where no returns are expected

Love is earthly, when it's beyond, it's much more than that . . .
And one only has to experience to know this, and perhaps, it
cannot be name or labeled, it is, just what it is.

That morning, beyond those leafs from the earthly pot over
the edge of my second floor of the towers of work, on the
floor well grounded to the earth was this person who had the
posture when he spoke on the phone, his white shirt, fitting
so well on his broad shoulders enhancing them, his khaki
trousers just fitting his waist, it was just the way he held his
phone and talked, he had a some grace around him, whatever
he just did, even when he did nothing at all, but just stood
there and spoke on that phone, holding in his hands . . .

I stood spell bound, overlooking through those green leave
over the earthen pot lines on the second floor and then looking
over the stair case and then on that ground, which resplended
with his presence, I could see him down there standing there
and it only when he, sort of, looked up, could I only see him
straight into his eyes and he into mine and no one could have
imagined that we could see so much of each other from the
ground floor on to the second floor, and me from second floor
to the ground floor diagonally opposite, it was that moment
that I captured in my eyes, with the white of his shirt over his
broad shoulder and his chest and he looked at me, with the
way you look at nature, his calm and his poise had gripped me
in those moments. Till I got caught in my own thoughts and

became conscious of myself looking over and went inside to continue my work in that towers . . .

For it sure was more than just being attracted to someone, when its more than just meeting up and talking up and sharing and looking forward to being together and just other normal progression of life.

Its routine, however, this was much more, cos everything else was, there, in life and this was building up by the side and naturally, by not talking but by being in the presence, by not waiting and looking forward to meeting but by just listening across the cubical, by not building up any expectations, but by just being soaked in that presence in that huge second floor, even if it far away . . . very far away, across all those cubicles, I felt that presence in that tower very strongly, more strongly than I ever felt than being in close quarters with any one else, it was this energy around him, when he walked in the second floor and went around talking to people for work, so deeply ingrained in work and yet so calm, so peaceful and so royal, without saying a word, it was, just his way, the way he walked down the ile, the way he did sat on the chair and the way he just looked over someone when he talked and I strongly felt his presence around, no matter what, as I lifted my head from I was sitting or used to be sitting or standing, it just did something inside, just lifting up my soul, my heart would smile, my soul would just energized. it was magnetic, in his presence, even if I noticed him from far away, I could feel his poise, his calmness, and somewhere a deep strong passion in him, it spoke more from the way he moved across and spoke to people, his undeterring way of talking, just looking straight into person's eyes, while he spoke, talked more of him than his words never falling into my ears, it did not matter what he said, how he delivered was, what caught me each time, I looked at him, and caught myself absorbed in him, completely and would just lift me up, would just induce energy in my fingers, to type with grit and strength, into my keyboards and words falling firmly on the screen of my computer

May be I saw someone on floor, who believed in himself and his principles more than I ever saw, may be I saw someone happy from within with what he was doing or delivering, may I saw someone who I could make out is happy and loved at home by his wife, that love and respect showed in his calm and respectful mannerisms, may be I saw someone who was more graceful than the any other achiever in a most healthy way.

May be I saw someone who carried deep involvement that for seconds together, it froze me, more than I thought, I would become like a statue and watch, not realizing that I was looking straight at him, may be it was his silence that spoke more than the words he uttered, may be it was just the way he saw up, once in a while noticing that I am noticing him, for he would acknowledge without saying a word, may be his eyes would convey much more than one need not talk . . .

And day after day, he would walk in any hours, with the phone in his hand and there was something about his walk and his aura that he left behind, I do not know how many really noticed this guy, I wonder if you will fail to notice this guy ever, the royal presence and the humbleness he had around him was something.

Anyone would fall for him, the way he would talk on his phone, his eyes so calm and his voice so firm, his posture so confident, there was something about this guy and each day it just pulled me in so much . . . it gave me strength day after day to have him around, I would only lift my eyes to notice his walking in, or may be when I was on landline, I would face the side where he would be standing, it could be far away, but I could make out the outline of his posture, his body, his broad shoulders, his neck, his ears, the way he wore his hair neatly and his little ring he would wear in one of his ear, never looking out of place, but fitting his whole personality so seamlessly, his movements and, I would watch till the time I could, till the time, my talk on phone could go on and on . . . there was something so strong about this guy, this soul, it gave strength, the thrill in my heart each day . . . His presence was enough, and that's it.

Times I would deliberately go after where by chance he would sitting and typing profusely on his computer. Times, I would stay back late, only cos he was around and then someone said, work stretches to fill the gap and my work would stretch to no limits, till he would be gone, and I would hear no more voice and all of a sudden my work would be over, there was nothing more to do, it was for the next day . . .

This went on for months and six months and one year, and two years and then three years and then four years . . . and our relationship in our eyes had grown. he had become aware of me watching him all these months and all these years, he had possibly also noticed my excitement in me whenever my gripped his presence, when he was around on the second floor, he noticed it, he had noticed every watching of mine in him, he noticed my movements changes when he was around, he had noticed every time, when I had just looked straight into him, holding me back, but looking into him intensely and very intensely into him, lest he had become conscious of others watching me looking at him, I did not care about others, watching me, he did.

Sometimes, my energy on seeing him was so strong, that he just completely avoided looking on my side, lest, I may greet him with all that energy in me.

It is a strange relationship, I feel strong, when I see him from a distance and its only when I am very very weak, do I have the need to get close to him, very close, he holding me, in the most cozy manner, my head on his broad shoulders, my lips touching his skin on his neck and his strong arms holding me up . . . to rub my shoulders against him, to get his strength in me, to get his posture in me, to feel his presence around me . . . and this was very seldom, for his presence made me strong, even in my own moments of being weak and not being good, of which he had no idea, he was not even aware of, but his just one glance towards me, made me strong, stand upright, it made my challenges look tiny, it gave life in me. and the relationship went on, in eyes, in the air, in the distance, and sometimes I feel, I have grown in this relationship, where we had just looked at each other, where we had only known that other was around, somewhere around, more so for me, I do not know, the story from the other side . . .

This was the soaking in this relationship, sans a word, sans a chat, sans being together, sans any exchange, sans any waiting, sans any expectation, sans any expression, sans any talk, sans everything, sans nothing at all . . .

To talk to him over the phone piece, once in a while from far away, very far away from the opposite corner of this city was like talking to him, on and on and his max sentence

would be . . . *"hmmmm" . . . what else . . . " . . . "ahhaa . . . "*
" . . . okayyy . . . " . . . "and . . . " and these would be his
long sentences and I would talk and talk, he would make me
feel as if by the end of the whole conversation, I had a lovely
exchange, with actually just me doing the talk . . . he would
make me talk, to him, I do not how, but I knew from the other
end, in the other corner of the world on the cell piece, would
be a person, is the person, who was sincerely listening to every
word of mine, who read in between the lines, who notices and
read my tone of talk and my breathe was also being heard, no
matter what, no matter how much it rained, or how much
traffic there would be . . ., whether he would be on the BEST
bus or driving back to his den on cordless phone, or with set of
people pooled to go back together, he listened to me.

And I spoke to him and in the end; still I had the best
conversation I have ever had, that's how he made me
feel . . . Once I had asked him, how can you listen to, so much
and he in the most calm, his usual way of talking, told me . . .
just the way, you can talk so much, I can listen so much . . .
and that he loves to listen, made me smile and mused at his
guy, what was he like, a rock by the side of shore, who listens
to so much gushing of waves all the time, and still, stays there,
listening and supporting and standing there like a rock and
yet, so unmoving. He was a rock . . . my listening rock.

No matter how tied up he was, in the middle of meeting or
discussion or wherever, he would always call back, if he was
not able to talk when I had called him, he would call back even
if it meant calling at 8.00 pm while on his way back . . . I was
amazed at his sensitivity or commitment; I did not know what
to name this . . .

And as the time passes by, and I get to see less and less of him, cos of some change of work roles, or perhaps a load of work . . . and whenever I see him, it seems to me watching my loveless living being infront of my eyes, my charatacter of my story so much in front of me, my numbness freezes, until, I have to lean to the wall I am standing close to, to believe to absorb and breathe, that I am actually watching him . . . a rarity, and see him growing better each day or may be he growing over me each day, how it becomes better and better and more graceful, this loveless relationship, where there is no relationship all, where, no returns are expected, where there is no love in return, for this is beyond the word called love, its lovesless . . . for the less I see of him, the reverse of what we used to say becomes more applicable . . . you heard this—out of sight and out of mind . . . here it is out of sight, and grows in mind, so much so that I have pinch myself to come out of trance to believe sometimes, when I see him, to see this rarity of human being, so much so that if I was a sculptor, I would have modeled him as a statue and would have carved every little details, so much so that if I was a salsa dancer, I would have passionately loved to dance with him, as if we were having the most high form of physical intimacy and yet so graceful and close, so much so that if I was a photographer, I would have captured his attitude on my camera, an attribute so rare, so much so that if I was a massager, I would taken sweet time, to touch every inch of his skin, spending a lot of time at every curve and skin . . . absorbing every inch

And I see less and less of him these days—to—seeing no more of him now, he does not even know this side of the story but then what the heck, this is one of very rare loveless tales . . . not to be told to the person about who is the censure of the story . . . ha.

Yet I am so thankful to the person of being around and make my day, thankful to him, to make my belief in seeing this person, that he believed in his principles, that he had an attitude with humbleness found so rare, that his face reflected a joy and love of his home and some peace on his face, meant so much more, meant how much a wonderful relation he must have had at home, meant how his wife possibly took care of him and he of her, it was written on his face, a face so calm and yet so passionate . . .

XLII.   Go to them, with Love and Respect and they will protect you

And whoever said that boys when in early twenties and teens become rash and run after women and the general sayings etc etc . . . for when I encountered what I encountered yesterday was the most respectful. Dressed up in my short skirt and shirt and my overcoat touching my ankles on a heavy rainy day, where the water was almost coming upto my knees and my jute bag, I am sure was touching the surface of water that was flowing profusely, while it was raining.

Yes, I did not have my stick umbrella, which I normally take to make sure of my road ahead, which flows with water knee deep, it helps me to wade the road and step forward and I did not have the same with me. I had to reach Andheri, anyhow, the goal had to be met, no matter what, it had to be done and someone had to do it, as simple as that. Its also funny, how much we love to do things for others, rather than for ourselves, it is most of the times this way.

Here I was walking out from my apartment and finding my way to the main road, with water filled and the road-ditches in middle, I do not know where . . . when I was walking or wading thru waters . . . these bunch of teenaged and early twenties boys and young men, were splashing over the water and stepping thru for water to go up in the air . . . is when one of them almost came infront of me while playing around, I asked him if he could walk me thru to the main road and I would just follow him he walked and I followed half way and he went away, then came another bunch of guys, playing thru water and I requested them earnestly, to walk me thru water . . .

They just agreed and started in line and I just followed them, the water was becoming deeper and I knew that further down, was somewhere a deep down ditch on road, perhaps they could sense my anxiety, they in the most natural way formed a V shape like the birds are, while flying and I walked in middle of that V shape, when we were on road, they asked me where do I have to go, knowing that I have to go to andheri, they just walked me about a mile to the bus stop, never asking me a question, why I am going, is it important, do I have to come back, it was the way it was, just it, no questions asked, these boys just guiding me to the right bus stop and asking, me to take the bus from there, it was in this middle of road, water logged that I almost slipped and held one of the persons hand firmly and he held mine, like he was wading a child thru the waters and we walked, I never looked up, looked down at water I was walking thru and just allowing myself to be followed by the person. we walked, it felt protected, like the, in nature from mother to child, that was the grip that said, and after sometime, when water was less, the grip loosed up and I was walking freely again, wow, I thought, and who are those people who say that the young boys have lost their decency, I came across the most respectful, protective and caring decency, I ever felt, in this city, this city is indeed amazing . . .

I was dropped at the bus stop, never could I look up, cos my cap of rain coat was big, but I just looked across those faces and said thanks and they returned, perhaps, happy, to have done some chivalrous work, I am sure they felt valued and I did feel honored.

Its strange in this world, when we ask for help, many, many come forward to give a hand, things we do for others, is sometimes just amazing and most of times, when we do things for others, is what brings us the most happiness . . . I still wonder why.

XLIII.   Body Massage

I go to know that massage is all about taking out the negative energies from the system and this definitely is an art, I also think not everyone can do a successful massage, it's all linked with how one thinks and what is the attitude of the person, it is also linked if the person has a loving and a caring heart.

Generally people who take life in a positive manner are also the person who are successful in transforming other people lives. It is about the vibes a person has around him or her. It's a capability which also can be developed. Human being would have this capability at its very basic level i.e. when human being at very very basic level of makes physical proximity or sex with one another, its all about, meeting the energies with one another and therefore, if you see there is lot of foreplay before the actual sex making, that's the time, when one of the person takes a lead in converting the energies into a more positive and an open one. There is a lot of hand massaging movements, to extend this further, this is done through using major sensual points like lips, the sensuous ones, the tip of fingers, the feet, the skin of the whole body, as it is during this process any obstructive energies in any one person is taken away, it is an art and surely that's why we see some people spending a lot of time in the foreplay, as it is during this foreplay, ones mind is getting prepared to accept the other person, therefore a good sex is when both the bodies have reached on the positive side and post that is the ultimate form of physical touch, which if we go to describe here will take us into a different realm of physical being or state

However, if only we could separate and concentrate on the physical touch part of any human being, we come back to our point that any kind of physical touch, in form of holding hands, or sitting next to each other with warmth or body massage comes primarily from removing or spreading ones positive vibes into another being or state.

That's how when a small baby is held, the physical touch is strongly recommended, with gentle massage movements on the baby, it takes away any fear or non positive energy from the baby. That's also when any head massage is given or any massage on feet is given and any body massage is given, the healing takes shape by physical touch of the hands and finger and palms. its also, as the body since childhood, has felt the most protective when touched, human being when they have this urge of getting touched physically explains that they are either feeling fearful or have some self doubts or are in need of physical reassurance for themselves, this is mostly related to how is the person's mind shaping up or feeling or has been feeling in that period of time or point of time.

The importance of physical massage or any physical touch healing is highly important as this leads to person feeling being loved, same way as when she or he was a child.

I consider body massage not only relaxing for the body but also, maintaining a healthy self esteem and a loved image for oneself. It also implies like in the beginning I said, taking away the negative vibes from the body, just as taking a bath is important to keep the body clean, it is essential for any human being to heal the body through healthy massage to wash away the negativity in the body and therefore the mind.

XLIV. At the International Airport

To disembark from the plane and pull the strolly bag along in the lobby of the airport in the place totally unknown, a land of outside region, where you are an alien, a foreigner, where no one knows you, where everything is new, is a feeling, where emotions are slightly mixed, where you have some excitement but at the same time, you are a little scared, where you look forward to meeting that someone special and yet, you are more excited cos you are in a new lands, you are a little lost and yet, you know, that you know someone here, and for that someone, you traveled the miles, for that someone, you crossed the oceans, for that someone, you flew the skies, for that someone you saved every penny, just to see him, just to hear his voice, just to spend some time with him, for sometime . . . just to look into his eyes. to love him, to feel him, to talk to him, to be with him . . . and you walk down that lobby in that international airport, feeling this, breathing this, holding this up and feeling graceful, loved, wanted, needed, peacefully impatient, to see your someone . . . you walk down that lobby of the airport, to have the coffee . . . to end those moments . . .

To sit in that place, where lamps glow in the most subtle manner, and where the lights fall on your face, so much that I can see that shine in your eyes, when you look at me that way, where, I smell flowers freshly plucked, where the music, makes me a little high, where, you come close to me, in the middle of nowhere, you hold my waist, like you hold the butterfly, with the fineness, you hold my hands and draw me closer to your chest, where you can hear my breathing, my heart beat goes a little more deeper and you hold me and grace my movements cn the music playing, where you dance with me with just looking into my eyes, and with every step, my breath goes deeper and I feel lighter and lighter . . . as if I am the clouds f.oating, as if I am the light falling like the moon, as if I am snow falling on a winter night, as if I am the leaf dancing and you are the wind holding me . . . and you parch me down on our table and we sit there, soaked in each other in our eyes is what I call being in your presence, in mine and in the lightlessness of being together . . .

To drive in that SUV, to go through the roads, through that upcountry, to handle the steering with you sitting next to me, to keep on driving and to pick up some thing on the way to munch, is what I call the drive, to drive it through . . .

And to sit in that verandah, watching the moon and the stars in the night, to feel a little chill of the night, to put my feet up on there and to nudge against you, in that big chair, is what I call blanking out at the night. To fall through the deep of the night . . .

XLV. Dreams are My Bridge to a conversation with Universe, My God

I think Dreams are the print out of what we think on a sub conscious level within ourselves. Dreams is the processed output of what we think on a very very sub conscious level, sometimes, we may not be even aware of same and we see them in dreams. I see that dreams are the most powerful language of gaining an insight to ourselves infact dreams are the way to signal us of what we are thinking and not even aware of sometimes.

Its like we have the waves of thought within us and when the antenna catches from within and while we are sleeping, we are in our senses not awake but our computer is working, I call this computer our brains and layers within our layers, its at this time that processing takes place and images are formed within and it comes as vision in our sleep which we call as dreams.

We have experiences in our lives all the time, the kind of emotions and physical level of waves our body goes through when we are awake and our sense are working, this is our internal system and then we have the external system to which our internal system responds and reacts all the time, this is the time, we are awake and are more or less aware of how we think, how we feel, emotions of happiness, anger, disgust and peace, all kind of emotions we go thru all the time and thus create waves of how we feel physically in our bodies, our body is only the mass that the waves of emotions goes, passes thru and thus out bodies gets effected, our hair, our skin, our face, our weight, our hands and legs, our back, our neck, our head, all in effected when these waves passes thru.

I⁻s when we are in state of sleep, we do not have the external environment not effect us, and that's when our internal system is completely in charge and responds completely of how we have been accumulating of what we think, or of what we feel, or are responding to in our minds and I think therefore that our dreams are more powerful as there is no external agency working in our body.

Dream therefore reflects of how are we feeling, what our major emphasis is, or what is impacting our minds most in life. Dreams could emanate from the feeling to do something powerful, or feeling of strong connect with God and some call it a powerful energy, or feeling of getting frustrated or angry over something that we do not like or is not in congruence to our thinking, or feeling of shear happiness and joy, or just being fearful of something in life. Dream reflect the same. When we listen to our dreams, we can also understand our deep deep human emotions and feelings that we are sometimes not even aware of.

Like I my dreams I have seen an ambassador car flying and it was quite nice to see that. I was going thru a phase in my life that time, when I was looking at achieving something which was not normal, out of reach and deep in my heart, I believed that this is possible, may be that's why I saw a dream like this. I also saw a dream where I saw a machine which was a combination of aircraft and train, it had lovely train bogies and it also had wings to fly, this is again connected to deep deep feeling of doing something which has not happened so far, and I can see it happening.

As child we have all seen dreams where we are either, slipping off or drowning or are running. This typically like many many interpreter have said is a feeling of being afraid or when we fear something. Then we also see people in our dreams, means we have been thinking about them in our lives and that when we see dreams, which are processing the data on sub conscious level.

I have seen dream of getting married to my best friend, and that it simply means of what I had been my dominant thought about this friend of mine, simple. I have seen many many dreams and so have you. I would only say, listen to what your dreams are telling you, there is message in the dreams that we see, and somehow I believe, Dreams are Gods way of talking to us, and we could become the person God has created for us to become, only if we listen to dreams and respect them and understand ourselves, better that we will ever get time for ourselves.

I therefore understand, how important our thoughts have to be and how we can link to what we think most of time by the bridge of our Dreams from our state to being Gods only person to carrying ourselves during the day to perform and live our lives each day, every day.

XLVI.   Un-concluded . . .

And in finally giving this book a shape, before it was to go to the publishing house, my friend asked me; Anita, have you given any conclusion, any closing to the book . . . I said no, nothing, it just ends as it is, no conclusions . . . and as I left that night, the night of Eid, in the local train at Matunga station, to which I walked some good 15 min, from dadar to matunga station to board the train to home. I thought to myself . . . conclusion, means ending and close . . . is this book a book about some kind of end to anything, anywhere, I don't think so, in fact this book for me, is the beginning yet again !!

As I read any book and complete it, I have either a new thought, or a new awareness, or even may be those thoughts were there in me somewhere, it just the book comes along and awakens me somewhere and I start to fly again, just like the butterfly out of a cocoon, which goes thru the process of transformation and in process grows into a lovely colored winged creation, to fly and experience everything, to touch and feel and know what is it to parch on flower and to sit on cactus and where-ever it likes and knowing it only by experiencing it, and the butterfly when it gets a fresh gush of wind from somewhere, it starts to fly again and this butterfly re-cocoons to become a more lovely creation, more than one time.

And the same has been with me, with every book, it has brought me closer to myself, there starts a new relationship with myself and like life its self is never ending, cos the soul always stays, it's the body, the face which changes, and the elements of nature, water, soil, fire and wind, again goes back to nature and then nature itself is always to be . . . like the planet earth, will stay, it may change its shape with times, it may take zillions of years, yet it shall be, and so does the galaxy and the universe, till we reach the infinite, there is no end, no conclusions . . . it only changes shape, and that's energy and the energy stays . . . forever in some form or the other . . .

And so I shall only say, there are no ends and no conclusions . . . These may be the seeds of new beginning on the continuum of experiencing and reflecting and moving . . .

Am glad you asked me, my friend!! Must I say thanks ☺

Some local terms that have been used in this book

Vadapav – local Mumbai fast food—an Indian burger (vada—mashed potato rolls. Pav-Indian Bun)

Cutting – slang used for half a cup of tea at local tea shops in Mumbai

Auto wala – three wheeler local transport in Indian cities and in Mumbai

Taxi Wala – Local Cab / taxi

Andheri – a porch suburb in Mumbai, name of a place in Mumbai

Matunga – another suburb in Mumbai, name of a place in Mumbai

Dadar – one of the main regions of Mumbai, one of largest railway station at the heart of Mumbai

Cos – the author liberally uses 'cos at different places in the book, which means because